The Stories We Leave Behind

A Legacy-Based Approach to Dealing with Stuff

Laura H. Gilbert

The Stories We Leave Behind
A Legacy-Based Approach to Dealing with Stuff
By Laura H. Gilbert

ISBN-10: 1981186018
ISBN-13: 978-1981186013
Published in the United States of America by CreateSpace,
June 2018.

Illustrations and cover design by Amanda Meador

To Our Stories

May they shine in the spotlight they deserve.

ACKNOWLEDGEMENTS

First, thanks go to Barbara O'Sullivan for encouraging me to share my experiences in book form.

Next, thanks to Sharon Brown from *Homescapes by Design*. You believed my quirky ideas were worth sharing and offered straightforward feedback that kept this book fun and practical.

A special thanks to Judi Kaper, Kim Vasquez, Lindsay Christensen, and Lesley Orr for your insights on storytelling, set design, staging and the art of prop selection. And a big thanks to Dane Stauffer and Park Square Theatre for creating a hands-on storytelling workshop for the 55+ crowd. Your timing and teaching are impeccable.

Many thanks to Monica Fisher, Tracey Baker, Lori Peterson, Steve Kuntz, Barbara O'Sullivan, Sharon Brown, Jennifer Anderson, Alex Liuzzi, and Beverly Pierce. This book is much stronger because of your insight, suggestions, edits and our lively discussions.

A big thank you to my friend Tamara Markus, problem-solver extraordinaire. Tammy stepped in at the last minute and worked some magic to get the final manuscript ready for press. Thank you!

Lastly, I'd like to thank Parichay Rudina and the caregiver support group at Wilder Foundation in Saint Paul. Your kindness and compassion remind overtaxed caregivers that our stories are also important.

TABLE OF CONTENTS

INTRODUCTION

The Stories We Leave Behind is a legacy-based approach to dealing with "stuff" in order to preserve our best stories and minimize the cleanup for loved ones after we're gone.

Everyone wants to be remembered well. We all have glory moments and ideals we hope will endure through stories told by friends and family: overcoming odds, being courageous, making a difference for a child or a cause. The legacy of our life lives on through these stories–our legacy stories.

Each of us will leave behind stories; and each of us will leave behind stuff. The clutter and chaos of a messy cleanup takes a toll on loved ones–be they adult children, nieces and nephews, or close friends–and shapes their final stories "with" us. Taking care of things now preserves the legacy stories we hope loved ones carry with them and, in the process, frees our time and space for today.

The Stories We Leave Behind asks the reader:

- How do I want to be remembered?
- How can cherished items highlight and preserve these stories?
- What can I do today to avoid leaving a burden of stuff for loved ones to deal with?
- Which stuff supports my life today?

The Stories We Leave Behind is not a one-and-done method but a process with a purpose. Step by step you'll uncover key stories, reduce stress for loved ones, and clear space for an environment that is truly you.

Although written from a baby boomer's perspective, this book is for anyone who wants to:

- Shape their legacy
- Embrace their encore years
- Reduce their volume of things in a meaningful way
- Avoid leaving a mess for loved ones

Benefits to you:

- You'll sharpen and position treasured legacy stories,
- Recapture time, energy, money and space for things you want to do,
- Distinguish stuff that supports your legacy or current life from stuff that doesn't, and
- Feel proud knowing you've made life easier for loved ones.

Benefits to your loved ones:

- Loved ones will be able to find and experience the legacy stories you want them to know,
- More time and energy can go to creating new memories and deepening your relationships,
- You'll provide an example for how to value AND let go of once-loved things, and
- You'll give your loved ones the gift of dealing with your own stuff.

PART I

Chapter One

LOST STORIES

"In life, every ending is just the start of another story."
Julian Barnes

Year by year, item by item, many of our homes become repositories for stuff. Our stuff, stuff from past generations, adult kids' stuff, stuff that seems to just appear. Good stuff, worn-out stuff, stuff we want, stuff no one wants. We've lost track of what we have and we can't find what we need. We feel guilty about the mess and guiltier about letting things go. Sorting, storing, shifting boxes, and protecting it all from mold or squirrels is a part-time job; a permanent task on the to-do list. At some point the stuff becomes our story.

Here is the story that led to this book–and how I reclaimed *my* stories, *my* time and *my* space and made sure loved ones would not be left with an unwelcome mess of stuff.

BACKSTORY

I could see it; the long-awaited light at the end of the tunnel. With the kids grown and retirement a decade or so away, I imagined sleeping in, exotic travel adventures, and ample "me time." Then life happened.

For years my aging parents struggled with stuff. To be fair they aren't hoarders. But they are second-generation, depression-era Americans who kept every single thing because "you never know–it might come in handy someday." Our musty basement was filled with outdated newspapers, unpopular canned goods, and odd-shaped boxes overflowing with mystery contents. Items were only released when "a good home" could be located.

Time and again, our visits included emotional appeals for me to take an item that "I know you'll want someday." These were not treasures. And to be clear, the intent was not to revive the *item* but rather to cherish and preserve *memories*; memories that meant more to them than to me. What they saw as a generous gift, I began to view as a burden.

Given my own full life, it was faster to smile and take the stuff than attempt reason and logic. Still, more than once a last minute change of heart meant items that had been painstakingly cleared for giveaway were kept because "we might still need it, but we'll keep it for you."

This pattern continued for many, many years. As other relatives died, my parents acquired their stuff too. Each visit was marked by more requests to "please help us deal with all this stuff."

Buried among the stuff they didn't want (but couldn't release) were remnants of their lives and their stories. My hope for each visit was to uncover cherished photos and items that told these stories; the stories my parents held most dear.

What was it like for Mom to be a Big Band musician on the road in all-girl groups? What insights about life and death could Dad share after 60+ years as a mortician? But as their health declined, a lifetime's worth of stuff remained the topic of conversation and a roadblock to action. "We'd move but we have all this stuff!"

Trip after trip I watched Mom agonize over each potential give-away, certain she "may need it someday" or that letting go would erase a memory and with it a little bit of her. On a good trip, three items were released: two to fly home with me because "one of your kids can surely use this" and a third to an understanding neighbor for a (non-existent) "collection."

As a mortician's daughter I was taught that funerals were the final chapter of one's life. But after Dad died, my parents' unfortunate connection to stuff became the final story, written as we faced the mess that was left behind.

From searching through drawers for time-sensitive burial documents to discovering prescription drugs in multiple locations; every drawer, box, and corner of their home was a potential hiding place for something important. The search took weeks. Exhaustion and stress usurped fond memories. Dad was a proud, happy man with a deep love for family and community. Clutter and stress were not the stories he intended to leave with us; but there we were.

Today, Mom remains alone in their home, paralyzed by her relationship with stuff; the dark, cluttered rooms of indistinct purpose a reflection of her growing depression. Try as I might conversations don't recall Mom's days on the road or life with Dad, but are consumed with her stress over stuff. Someday good stories may return, but they will forever be colored by the personal impact of all that stuff.

The last few years took a physical, emotional and financial toll on me that I would not wish on anyone. Deep and relentless stress impacted home and work. Eventually I quit my job. I reasoned that devoting myself full-time to addressing my mother's situation would bring a resolution and allow me to get back to my job and my life.

I was wrong. No matter what I did or how hard I tried her inability to deal with stuff remains the impenetrable road block to healthy action and happier days.

NOT TO MY LOVED ONES!

One day, while sitting on the floor of my living room after a particularly difficult visit, I hit a wall. I was exhausted and emotionally drained. I had done all I could and then some, as had the grandchildren and a dear niece. Neighbors, friends, clergy, medical professionals, even a banker urged me to take care of myself while also insisting I "do something" to transition Mom to a safer, simpler life. But as unhappy as Mom was, she would have none of it. There was nothing anyone could do to alter Mom's self-imposed situation–ever.

It was also clear we would never chat about her life or her stories from the road. Ironically her most cherished stories, the ones I'd gotten glimpses of in the past, were fading while she was still alive and mentally sharp. Sadly, her final stories, the stories we will carry, will not be about family, or love, or even her career in music, but about her dilemma with stuff.

This was NOT the experience I wanted for my loved ones, nor for my own final years. I'm what my son calls an "upbeat" person, cup-half full. The last thing I wanted to do was slip into negativity, dragging down friends and family, especially if that negativity was over stuff. Nope.

And I didn't want my stories to get lost in unnecessary chaos.

I vowed then and there to avoid leaving a similar experience for my family. I would not let my stuff become their burden.

I would not spend my final years begging them to take things. Nor would our final story be about a stressful cleanup.

Instead, I would find a way to embrace the stories I most wanted to leave behind; stories of hope and love and family; stories that affirm rather than burden. And I would make those stories obvious, easy to know and easy to find in my space.

Fired up for action, I was ready to craft a plan to ensure this outcome. I was already a relentless downsizer. Key documents were "in order." There was still stuff to sort through but this new perspective was about more than volume reduction and organized closets.

It was about the final chapter of a life lived, a message sent, relationships embraced–a legacy; *my* legacy.

It was about the stories I wanted to leave behind.

I thought about the cherished memories I held of a favorite uncle and a best friend. How do I describe them? What stories are retold by others who knew them? Some stories tell of a special event while others speak to a personal achievement. Each story reflects who they were, what they meant to me, and how they made me feel. Beyond an item here or there, these stories preserve their legacies.

I wondered about the stories I might leave for those I hold most dear. How could I make sure treasured stories weren't lost in the final cleanup? Decluttering and downsizing address volume, but I wanted more. I needed a new approach.

What if I were to start with the ideal end?

I threw a virtual "Hail Mary" to the universe. What would the ideal end look like? Sound like? Feel like? What did I really want loved ones to carry with them after I'm gone?

Stories. Good stories. Stories that shared lessons and values I hoped to pass on. Stories about the people and experiences I held most dear. An abundance of happy memories of our final years ("Mom lived life to the very end.") In the end, my end, I knew I wanted to leave a legacy of strength and hope; a legacy that left those closest to me feeling undeniably loved.

I imagined a final cleanup that would be the stage for the stories I hoped to share. What would the cleanup look like? Sound like? Feel like? Smell like?

The scene was clear.

Meet at Mom's place around 8 with donuts and coffee. Reminiscing, laughter, tears, more laughter (probably 80's dance music in the background). Explore rooms, closets and shelves. Pause to smile or chuckle over a trinket discovered here, a special book found there. Decide which stuff to keep, toss or donate. Angela (the firstborn) would create the list. Go to lunch. Done. Yep, done. A half day...Well ok, they'll be time to box stuff, arrange for pick up and probably mop, but the hard part– identifying what was there and making distribution **decisions** *–was done in a warm, supportive, roughly half-day experience with its own positive, affirming, and hope-filled memories; before they got glossy-eyed and grumpy* ☺

And there it was.

THE DISCOVERY HALF-DAY

I loved it. Big decisions made in about a half day, bookmarked by food and fun time for remembrance and stories–the best stories, legacy stories, the stories I left behind. No clutter. No random piles of stuff. Instead of adding to their grief with a big mess, I could hear the laughter and imagine the stories.

"Remember the time when…" The joy was palpable. This was the ideal cleanup scenario I wanted for my loved ones.

Getting there would take time, but the idea of a discovery half-day provided a goal that could help me preserve my best stories and minimize cleanup decisions. Best of all I would start from a place of joy and affirmation. Instead of reliving personal shortcomings and lost dreams, I would search for the wins; the best parts of my life, the stories I hope lift up loved ones or offer encouragement long after I'm gone. ("You're great-grandmother did [fill in the blank.] You can too.") These are the stories I want them to find.

The more I thought about it, a half day made sense. Even enjoyable activities get tedious after a while. Plus, human attention is truly limited.[1] Prized stuff and stories must stand out to be preserved. Highlighting a handful makes them special – and discoverable.

Plus young families are strapped for time. Loved ones often live in multiple states. Devoting a weekend to fly in and close up a loved one's residence is a reasonable expectation:

- 4 hours to sort stuff and make initial decisions
- 8 hours to pack and arrange pickups
- 4 hours to clean the place for sale or a new resident

Sorting through a loved one's stuff is difficult in the best of circumstances. Minimizing this task feels respectful and kind –as long as important stories are preserved.

---

[1] "The **average attention span** for the notoriously ill-focused goldfish is nine seconds, but according to a new study from Microsoft Corp., people now generally lose concentration after eight seconds, highlighting the effects of an increasingly digitalized lifestyle on the brain." May 13, 2015
https://www.google.com/search?q=attention+span&ie=utf-8&oe=utf-8&client=firefox-b-1

PERSONAL REWARDS

It's been more than a year since I began to work toward creating a discovery half-day for my loved ones. The positive impact has gone far beyond minimizing cleanup and highlighting stories.

- I got unstuck
- I gained clarity about the legacy I hope to leave
- I rediscovered important stories from my past
- I let go of once-loved stuff that might distract from more meaningful stories
- I experienced more calm and joy in my own space
- I freed up my time (& money) to explore new interests
- I found space for stuff that aligns with current and growing interests
- I had great conversations with people from multiple generations about legacy and stuff
- I learned how much my family appreciates this work

Occasionally I stand at my front door and ask, "Could the kids actually make decisions about this stuff in a half day AND experience the stories I want them to remember, the values I want them to know?"

At other times I simply review categories of stuff (e.g., kitchen, books, photos) and ask, "Could the kids make decisions about *this category of stuff* in a half day AND is it laid out to tell a story I want to tell?"

Either way, the idea of a half day for discovery and decisions helps me select stuff to showcase my best stories–my legacy stories–for tomorrow and today.

Here's what the alternative can look like. But first a quick note: the role of "kids" in this story is frequently played by nieces and nephews, cousins, or close friends. Insert the loved ones who are likely to be your final cleanup crew.

Rick and Maggie are typical baby boomers. They have a big house that currently holds three+ generations' worth of stuff: their stuff, inherited stuff, and stuff stored for young adult children, all of it mixed together. Stuff that currently impacts their life. Too much stuff to make it easy to move. So, they keep it. Time goes by. Maggie dies, followed a couple years later by Rick.

If their home stays as is until Rick's death, their three adult children will face the disposition of everything in the house; a task that will cost time, energy and money for cleanup specialists, haulers, and dumpsters to name a few. A task that must occur before the house can be sold, which means continuing to deal with and pay for property taxes, insurance, routine maintenance and yard care, basic utilities (e.g. heat in cold climates so the pipes don't freeze), and the ever-present but unplanned house-related expenses (tornado damage, leaky roof, critters).

All three adult children have busy careers and home lives. Two of the three have young children. Did I mention they live in three different states? Their employers offer the standard three days of bereavement leave. That's five days if you include a weekend. One to fly in and hold a wake. One for the memorial service. One to fly home. That leaves two days to deal with urgent, immediate details and plan the cleanup.

They will likely schedule the home cleanup event for a weekend to minimize travel expenses and time away from work and home. A weekend gives them a few hours to make core decisions and the bulk of the time to implement those decisions (pack, ditch, arrange pickups), and a few hours to actually clean.

Given the way things were left and their personal time constraints, Rick and Maggie's kids may have already resolved to simply toss everything into a dumpster (or two or three), and perhaps find a treasure or two along the way.

This is sad and hard. Happy stories are overshadowed by the story of the big cleanup. Rick and Maggie's kids loved their parents. But they need to get back to their own lives, the lives Rick and Maggie raised them to live. This is not a burden Rick and Maggie intended to leave.

Now imagine if Rick and Maggie were present at the weekend cleanup. Assuming a half-day attention limit before stuff just gets tossed, what would Rick and Maggie make sure was not overlooked or misunderstood? What stories would they want the kids to discover, to be reminded of, to take with them? What would they most want the kids to notice from their parents' lives? Rick and Maggie's answers could provide the basis for a much different experience; one in which that precious weekend includes time to reminisce, grieve and start the healing process. One that reflects the final stories Rick and Maggie want to leave for their kids.

NOT ALONE

The truth is, many of us have some version of "sort through stuff" on our to-do list. Whether it's three storage units full of stuff or a few lingering stashes to "get to someday" stuff takes up our time, our energy, and our money.

Keeping everything wasn't a problem for past generations. But today we seek simplicity and flexibility–not easy if you have tons of extra stuff. And, while Baby Boomers talk about how to get rid of it, GenXers and millennials talk about how to not take it. Specifics vary but the challenge is the same: what to do with all the stuff that no one wants.

Last spring I went to a discussion on transitioning to the encore life–a popular baby boomer view of retirement. Dealing with decades of stuff was a shared challenge. Stuff was taking up time, energy and space that these bright, action-oriented problem-solvers would rather spend on new adventures, honing one's legacy, or reading a book by the lake. The next generation doesn't want it yet we feel responsible to care for it–even though its useful days (or original owners) are long gone. This group was about embracing the future and our stuff was holding us in the past.

I understood. I'd been there. And at my lowest point I had discovered a quirky approach that helped me break free. As an introvert I tend to nod and smile in groups rather than make bold statements. But I was compelled to share. I took a deep breath and asked, "Do you want to hear about my discovery half-day?"

I figured if nothing else, that statement alone would break the tension with a laugh. It did. And then the mood shifted and with it the discussion.

The idea of preserving our stories while minimizing a loved one's cleanup was compelling. But was a half day impossible? What was included? Were there exceptions?

I explained that the discovery half-day was about major decisions and human attention span, especially in the face of grief. Faced with a major cleanup task, how long before our best stories, our legacy stories, meld into the background and it all becomes a pile of stuff? Everyone had stories to preserve, a legacy to share. What could we do today to make those stories shine?

We agreed legacy went beyond the property and money one might bequeath. Many of us had experienced job loss, the market crash, an unexpected medical crisis, or caregiving for an elderly parent–all events that impacted our savings and downstream inheritance for loved ones or charities.

But each of us had life stories in abundance. Stories of courage, persistence, and community. Stories that passed on life lessons, values, heritage. Stories that came from making a difference. Stories we wanted to pass on. And stories we wanted to avoid creating, such as being a burden to loved ones in our final years or leaving a messy cleanup.

Our interests were consistent whether we had many children or none; were married or single; were a socialite or a hermit; had ample retirement funds or none. Everyone had stories. Everyone had stuff. Everyone had a legacy to preserve.

Since then, I've often been asked to talk about the discovery half-day. I've also had eye-opening discussions about stuff with GenXers and millennials. Reasons vary but the response is the same: a firm "no thank you" to relatives eager to pass along stuff, and a longing to replace stuff-centered conversations with deeper, more meaningful family dialogue.

With every conversation I'm reminded just how big, and how common, this task is.

Chapter Two

THE STORY OF STUFF

"Where did you get all this stuff, Grandma?"
Hazel, 3 years old

So…if stuff overshadows our best stories, takes our time, and threatens to become a mess for others to clean up, why can't we just sell it, donate it or ditch it? What invisible strings latch things tightly to the floor as we scan through items? Has anyone else ever sensed an occasional Jedi wave, followed by a soft "These are not the items you want [for the garage sale]."

Tired of arguing with myself over which item was a keeper and which one wasn't, I paused. How did we get here? More specifically, how did all this stuff get here? I had lots of crabby answers but the fact is this wasn't all junk. Even though its time had come, it deserved some respect.

Originally each item was purchased, made or gifted for a purpose. Some by me, some by my kids, some by my parents, some by friends, and some by ancestors I never met. Together these items represented wildly different times in history, social norms, economic conditions, needs and stories.

It seemed only right to pause and reflect on the broader journey of this collective stuff. Doing so deepened my understanding and sensitivity to the challenge we face.

A Brief History of Stuff

The baby boom generation includes people born between 1946 and 1964. That means our depression-era parents were born 80-100 years ago (give or take). Stuff was scarce.

Further, many of our parents were born to immigrants who arrived at Ellis Island[2] with their parents in search of economic opportunity–and the material prosperity they hoped would follow. They arrived with little. Each item that survived the long and treacherous journey was precious; a fleeting connection to family they might never see again.

As time went by those early families worked hard to gather stuff; needed stuff, special stuff. Stuff that was theirs. Signs of the "better life" they sought. When a child married or a parent died, stuff was passed on to the next generation as a symbol of love, generosity and heritage–to "remember us by."

This tradition was repeated over and over, with each generation adding its own stockpile to the mix. Gradually, personal connections to stuff and the ability to acquire things changed.

After two world wars and a devastating depression, the economy was finally strong. The next twenty years were a time of growth and innovation. 1950s suburbia offered millions of middle-class families a first chance at the American Dream: their own house on their own land. Homes were furnished with the latest and greatest stuff: automatic

---

[2]"On April 17, 1907, an all-time daily high of 11,747 immigrants received is reached; that year, Ellis Island experiences its highest number of immigrants received in a single year, with 1,004,756 arrivals."
http://www.history.com/topics/ellis-island# last accessed February 7, 2018

washer and dryer, television, dishwasher, and so forth. Many of us were raised in these homes. Homes we, too, filled with stuff.

And as we know, human nature can drive us to want more than the other guy, regardless of need, especially when success is measured in stuff. The term "keeping up with the Joneses" became a thing, and with it the gathering of more stuff. Nonessential and "newfangled" stuff. Stuff met by Grandpa's disapproval, as in "You spent good money on THAT?!" But stuff that made our parents feel successful and made us feel normal in comparison to classmates.

Time passed. More and more stuff was purchased or passed down. At some point society shifted from need-based purchasing to full-fledged consumerism. A thing exists so I want one (or in marketing terms "the thing exists so you need one to be happy or cool or successful"). The new motto was: "He who dies with the most toys wins."

Houses (and garages) expanded to hold all the stuff. Storage facilities popped up. And all the stuff was kept. As our parents' generation began to pass, so did their stuff–to us. Good stuff, broken stuff, outdated stuff. Generations' worth of stuff. And while our dad may have inherited his father's toolbox, this same 1950s collector Dad may leave us with Grandpa's tool box AND a tool shed, workshop, and garage.

Family stories began to get lost among the clutter. Grandpa's toolbox, as a single, special inheritance held precious family stories while most items in Dad's shed/workshop/garage were indistinguishable from those of any other neighbor. But every item was kept–regardless of condition or usefulness–because "I might need it someday", or "Someone could use this", or "This belonged to your Great Grandma", or "I paid a lot for this!" or my favorite, "Someone could make something out of this."

One thing for sure. All that stuff meant far more to them than it means to many of us–let alone the next generation.

Eventually we added our own stuff to the mix. Lots and lots of stuff; for us, our kids, our descendants, and even our pets. If that sounds over the top, I ask you: What were Fido's possessions in 1955? A food bowl, a dog house, an old tennis ball, a bone, all kept outside–right? How does this compare with your three-year-old grand dog Bailey? (Pause) Ok, now think about "essential" baby stuff then and today. How much lives in your house today, ready for visitors? Mine too.

IF THERE'S ANYTHING YOU WANT…

So here we are, our encore years rapidly approaching, surrounded by stuff. Our stuff, possibly kids' stuff, parents' stuff, long-gone relatives' stuff; stuff we don't even recognize. Stuff we want, stuff we don't want, stuff with emotional value, stuff with dubious value, and an item here or there with monetary value–maybe. Spending our free time sorting through stuff is not the encore life we envisioned.

Unfortunately, it's too late to send most stuff back from whence it came (be it the 1890s or the 1990s). And, unlike our parents, we can't pass it on to the next generation because:

- ➢ They don't want it, and
- ➢ They don't feel an obligation to take it

Why? Because, simply put, how we "do" life has changed.

The next two generations (GenX: born 1965-1980 and millennials: born 1981-1996), and their kids, (GenZ: born 1996-2012 and Gen Alpha: born 2013-2030) were raised in a different world than were their parents and grandparents. Thus they approach life quite differently than earlier generations.

Their world is digital and virtual

- We built cardboard models; they interact with 3D holograms
- We wrote letters; they Facetime (or something newer)
- We used maps; they ask Siri
- We made our own pizza from scratch; they order delivery via "Ask Alexa"
- We fixed broken things; they upgrade
- We made footprints in the snow; they have digital footprints
- We grew up with stand-alone technology (transistor radio, electric typewriter); they have integrated systems (smartphones include a phone, camera, music, movies, internet and apps to do almost anything).
- Old stuff doesn't work in their world. Grandma's dial phone was still usable when we got it. Today it's either a conversation piece or just old.

Their world is global and ever-changing

- Younger generations are independent and global. We moved around the neighborhood. They move around the world.
- Their work world moves at the speed of light. Their grandparents built toward one career. They expect to have many.

Their relationships are nearby (albeit electronically)

- As a 1950s era kid, one of my grandmas lived 5 hours away, which meant I saw her once or twice a year.

The other lived in Arizona. We visited her twice—ever; three long days each way via train with a final bus ride through the desert (without air conditioning).

We never spoke on the phone due to cost, party lines, etc. We kept in touch through occasional postcards and a few cherished pictures, each of which meant something because it was all we had. Those items represented our relationship; and I still have them.

- In contrast, I can Facetime with my grandson in Europe *for free*, share photos from the moment, or send money he can access in seconds. He can literally call me from a café, and I can transfer funds he can access by the time he reaches the register – across the ocean. I can practically smell the coffee.

Should we wish an in-person visit, reasonably-priced flights leave daily between our cities. He doesn't need a "thing" to remember me or feel loved. We have technology.

Maybe one thing…

To be fair, the next generation may want ONE item, especially if it's a novelty item or conversation piece. But as with my grandson, they aren't inclined to connect love for a person to a thing. To experiences, yes. To memories, yes. Things, not so much.

What they DO want

There are some things they do want.

- *They want us–their parents and grandparents–to be happy.* To have a good life. To be active and live our lives to the fullest for as long as possible.

- *They want to hear our best stories, wisdom and insights.*

- And, just like we taught them to do, *they want us to take care of our own stuff.*

Like it or not, you and I know all too well what that means:

The proverbial ball (or truckload of stuff) has landed firmly in our court.

THE BUCK (AND HUTCH) STOPS HERE

So what does it mean for us to be the final resting place for generations' worth of stuff?

In plain terms it means:

Baby boomers are where the buck (and hutch) stops.

Consequently, we are the transitional generation for the role stuff plays in families.

Generations before us passed things along as remembrance, assistance, and love. Generations after us want stuff that supports an interest, need, or lifestyle of their choice. Little of our stuff fits that bill.

Thus, like it or not, we must make decisions we'd hoped to pass on to younger generations, including decisions older generations left for us. Does this feel heavy? It is. Unfair? It is. This is a responsibility we didn't expect or volunteer for.

If decision-making is not your thing, this could be an extra tough challenge, especially when letting go makes you feel like judge and executioner of your ancestors or family memories. Even if you're cheering at the realization that this truly is all "yours" to do with as you will, there is still stress.

There's a daily impact on your time and space and an energy drain from unfinished business and recurring cleanup efforts. Costs can add up to store, move, care for, or to sell, give away or dispose of items. Stress may impact your job, relationships, and emotional or physical health.

Don't be surprised if you feel sad, frustrated, anxious, guilty, ashamed or even angry at some point. You may even experience feelings of loss on someone else's behalf. For example, personally I'm fine giving away Grandma's old teapot but I'd feel terrible knowing how upset she would be. It is not a loss to me but it would be to her; a loss I carry forward in her absence, waiting for permission to let it go which she can never grant; a loss replete with guilt for even thinking about putting it in the giveaway pile.

On good days I imagine asking Grandma, standing there in her flour-covered apron, if she would really want this teapot to cause me this much stress. If phantom Grandma says "Ditch it, Honey!" it's gone. If she delivers a guilt trip I take a deep breath–and put it in the giveaway pile. Do whatever it takes to give yourself permission to let these items go. Brush off any lingering guilt dust and move on. This is your life. Live it.

Being the transition point for stuff, especially old or sentimental stuff, is hard. But baby boomers are tough. We embraced life, were all we could be, came a long way baby, rode the technology tsunami and did it our way. We raised families and built careers–sometimes more than once. We are change makers, leaders, and survivors. And we truly hope to make a difference in the world. We can do this too.

And in the process we'll leave an incredible gift–and model– for generations to come.

WHY DOWNSIZING, DECLUTTERING AND ORGANIZING FALL SHORT

You may be thinking, "Isn't this just downsizing, decluttering and organizing?" Yes and no. If you're like me you've purchased multiple organization "systems", spent weekends decluttering and are on a first name basis with Goodwill employees. Yet something is still unfinished. Why?

Downsizing, decluttering and home organizational techniques measure success by volume and order rather than how items might be used to preserve your legacy stories. The difference starts with the initial sorting question: "Does a lamp highlight this legacy story?" rather than "Which lamps can I let go of?"

21

It may be important to reduce volume and increase order. If so, be prepared to face some emotional decisions. This is more than pulling random weeds. This is stuff someone (possibly us) wanted, chose, bought or handmade with a specific purpose or person in mind.

Letting go may come with feelings of grief, loss and self-doubt; feelings that sap energy and leave us feeling drained. The resulting emotions can range from tiny, "Maybe I shouldn't have given away the bag of old file folders" to immense, "What if Great Grandpa's old brown jug is like the one on Antique Roadshow! What have I done!?" Even the fear of those feelings can weigh down decisions.

In contrast, asking which items highlight a legacy story is positive. The entire purpose is to tell your story in a way that's true to you and compelling to loved ones. Once your story is exactly how you want it, with the items you believe best bring that story to life, everything else is less important. Not "not important." Just less so. From there, downsizing and decluttering isn't so much about letting go but more about shining the spotlight on your favorite stories–and clearing the rest off the stage.

Without asking the legacy question first, it's possible to end up with highly organized stuff that doesn't feed your life and leaves a nondescript story–Mom had stuff and it was in order, period.

Personally, I didn't just want less stuff in good order. I wanted to preserve my best stories, prevent a messy cleanup and live out my life with room to breathe. I needed to feel confident about choosing stuff to keep and choosing stuff to let go of. That required knowing first what I wanted in a bigger sense.

WHAT DO WE WANT?

Our ancestors intended to be generous and kind by passing on their stuff. And we recognize there are rational, logical reasons why the next generation doesn't want it. But…

What do we want?

Not what <u>stuff</u> do we want but what do we want the *rest of our life* to be about? What do we want life to look like on a daily basis? What would make us, or more specifically you, happy?

Three themes come up over and over with baby boomers who face a houseful of stuff. Baby boomers want to:

1. Leave a legacy

Be it for a child or the earth, we want to leave a legacy.

Past generations worked toward legacies (aka an inheritance) of property, stuff, and money (as in Billy gets the farm). Baby boomers as well as GenXers and millenials want to be remembered for more. We want to make a positive, lasting difference; to feel our life mattered–somehow, somewhere in the grand scheme of things. Nowhere is this more important than with our loved ones–be they children and grandchildren, nieces and nephews, siblings, good friends, or a valued charity. And that happens through stories.

2. Avoid leaving a mess for loved ones

Whether through personal experience or watching a friend struggle with a loved one's estate, we know we do not want our loved ones to face a messy and expensive cleanup. Nor do we want our most cherished stories to get lost. When the time comes, we want loved ones to be able to remember the good times, grieve, heal and move forward.

We also want this for us because it feels like the right thing to do. We want loved ones to feel good about how we left things. And we want to be a role model for letting go of things and for living life full out to the very end.

3. *Embrace our encore years*

This is OUR TIME. After decades of taking care of business (and family and homes and and and...) it is our turn.

This is a chance for a new beginning complete with new stories and new memories. Fun, learning, creativity, adventure, family–whatever you want to try or do within rational means (as defined by you).

Health or unexpected family needs may put a hiccup in these adventures, but possessions need not get in the way. The plethora of 55+ travel groups, art courses, college course offerings and so forth speak to the growing array of baby boomer interests and opportunities. We are not done.

Chapter Three

CHOOSING AND TELLING
LEGACY STORIES

"As we age, we have a single duty and that is to tell our stories."
Guillermo Del Toro

Whether or not we acquire wealth or fame in our lifetime, one thing is certain: we all have stories. Stories we lived and stories we carry from past generations. When we leave this earth others will remember us through these stories.

When I survey my stuff I see lots of stories I'd like loved ones to remember. Some reflect times together (family trips), some are just about me (returning to college as an adult), and some are about values I tried to practice along the way (respect, support, persistence, or simply "make time for fun").

But family and friends have their own lives and their own stories. My stories are simply one chapter–or more likely a paragraph–in their lifetime of stories. Which is as it should be.

Whether loved ones remember one story or ten, it certainly won't be all of them. And while I can't choose how someone might remember me, I can highlight the stories I most hope live on in their chapter of me. These are my legacy stories.

WHAT IS A LEGACY STORY?

Legacy stories collect the memories of our life for others to carry forward. As such, legacy stories typically:

- Evoke feelings or memories about an individual

- Are relatively few in number—with fewer and fewer recalled over time

- May be remembered a bit differently by each loved one who shares in it

- Are told over and over

Legacy stories are not bound by subject, time, or how widely they are known. They include stories one intends to leave behind and stories long forgotten that made a mark in a loved one's memory.

A legacy story might emerge from a lifelong interest, a deeply held value, one's career or volunteer activities, or simply from a big personality. Together these stories reflect who we were in the world and for the world.

Each of us has a few stories we hope family and friends remember long after we're gone. Many of those stories are reflected in our stuff: the cake plate used for 40 years of birthday celebrations, the cherished collection of mystery novels, a great uncle's watch.

When that stuff gets mixed in with clutter and the practical stuff of daily life, legacy stories get lost. Doing what we can to highlight this stuff preserves our stories, prevents a messy cleanup for loved ones, and frees up time and energy for today.

In search of examples

There was one more thing I needed before selecting my stories: examples. I wondered if there was a pattern to stories that live on? Shared elements? I thought about family stories told of loved ones long gone. I read tips from non-profits that help seniors tell their life story (in writing or film). And I listened to others reminisce. Three broad storylines emerged:

Some stories described a single item, event, or recurring events:

- "This is the cake plate from Grandma and Grandpa's wedding."
- "Here's the program from the day Mom earned her degree."
- "This picture reminds me how Grandpa would play catch with me every time he visited."

Some stories communicated personal traits or values:

- "Marguerite filled every room with laughter."
- "June was such a kind and generous person who made everyone feel welcomed."
- "Uncle Roger exercised first thing each morning."
- "Dad valued family above all else."

Some stories illuminated a vocation, volunteer work, or hobbies:

- "I loved hearing how Aunt Ruth worked her way up from mail "girl" to vice president."
- "After Velma died, Bill led international exchange programs for their favorite charity."
- "Great Grandma was always quilting for somebody!"

Three to five themes

Each story also reveals a theme that defined or shaped someone's life. Remembering a theme opens the door to many sub-stories that reinforce the theme. For instance, "Aunt Betty loved to entertain" expands to "Remember her annual holiday part? The smell of fresh-baked pecan pie, the carefully decorated tree, and the sound of Bing Crosby on the stereo?" or "She was so proud when the local news did an article about her cookbook." Story upon story upon story under a common theme–entertaining with food.

Themes also bring to mind different sub-stories for different loved ones. Daughter Sandy remembers the rich smell of Aunt Betty's pot roast dinner for fifty while cousin Buck chuckles as he recalls the 4th of July fiasco when Aunt Betty's ice cream cakes melted (after 7-year old Buck mistakenly took them out "to thaw"). Great niece Casandra remembers one-on-one time with Aunt Betty as they rolled dough for gingerbread men cookies for her Girl Scout troop (the irony not lost on Casandra). The stories vary but the theme is the same.

As generations pass, themes linger more than specifics. A few themes. Maybe three to five. Our big themes. Family, adventure, public service, courage. Perhaps being a war hero or a lifelong musician. Maybe sports played a central role throughout your life–or volunteering for a special cause. However and wherever we've lived our lives, we'll likely be remembered by a variety of stories that speak to a few broad themes.

And that's enough.

A couple years ago I lost a dear friend. When I think of her legacy to the world three to five broad themes come to mind with hours of related stories. Mutual friends add their stories under the same themes. When I think of friends or relatives who've been gone 30 or more years I can share my memories in a few sentences and perhaps one personal story. Although many stories faded away their life themes still shine through.

For example, my Great Aunt Ellen was a working woman, a staunch Baptist and a champion for worker's rights. Her clutter-free home and perfectly starched blouses reflected high standards for tidiness and practicality. Conviction and strength were core themes of her life.

One story passed down by her nephew (my uncle) is locked in our family history. Though small in stature and well past retirement Aunt Ellen brought a shareholder's meeting to its knees when she respectfully raised a well-hidden contractual promise that saved retiree benefits. In one legacy story Aunt Ellen's life themes come to life for generations to follow.

I wondered…what were my themes?

UNCOVERING THEMES AND STORIES

Not surprisingly stories were everywhere. Some stories were clearly more important than others; far too many to absorb in a half-day discovery event. And frankly, some stories had outlived their time and were just taking up space.

I needed to start somewhere fast or risk being paralyzed by the enormity of the task. I scanned the room. What were my big themes?

I saw the stuff of well-worn family tales shared with newbies to include them in our family culture: '80s DVDs from which many family one-liners originated; unseasonably hung blinky lights reminiscent of home dance parties. And, honestly, some parts of my space said little more than "someone lives here."

The real gems were stories tied to early dreams and achievements; stories that instantly reminded me who I was, and had always been. Rediscovering these stories was deeply affirming. A couple were important stories that had taken a back seat (or attic box, if you will) to life.

One such story had been hidden on the shelf for years. As I scanned with new eyes, I saw a manila envelope poking out between two books. I'd noticed it before but this time I paused and looked.

Inside were long forgotten professional photos of an annual flute festival I led during my first career as a musician. Each year I felt I'd made a difference simply by creating this opportunity for students and families. But then I left music and built a whole other career (a couple actually). Other than the presence of my instruments and a shelf of untouched music, memories of that decade were relegated to storage. A rush of memories came back as I browsed through the photos – and it felt like home. In an attempt to find my legacy stories I had rediscovered a piece of myself I wanted to bring back.

In the end the festival story itself wasn't important, but the overarching theme of my life as a professional musician was. The story could be brief but I wanted loved ones to know the depth of my career; that I attended a conservatory, performed in various venues, taught at national workshops, played for Rampal–and created and ran the festival. That sentence alone is enough to deliver the theme and the message I hope to share: embrace your dreams.

Another clear theme in my space was family. Unlike music, family has always been visible in my life. There are photos on the walls, a small bookshelf of individualized photo albums, and samples of artwork and trinkets gifted by family members through the years. A child's corner with a drawing table, art supplies and chairs that reflects the relationship I share with my grandkids.

But what about "family" did I want my loved ones to feel, to take from my life–from our time together? What values, lessons or experiences did I most want them to be able to use in their own lives? What stories best delivered that message?

Personal values, important lessons and key experiences came to mind: each of you matters just as you are; family sticks together when the going gets tough; remember the lifelong impact of special times with our dearest friends. And then I realized I didn't care so much about the *events* loved ones remembered, but I did care about the feelings and lessons that grew from the events.

I *did* want them to feel valued and loved. I *did* want them to feel confident they could count on each other. And I *did* want them to recognize there were others out there who valued and loved them too; examples of how they, too, might brighten someone else's world.

And if that's all they carry forward in regards to family…it is enough. Anything more is bonus.

In that moment I discovered the *essence* of the family theme for me, and with it the core messages I wanted to leave behind. This was a huge breakthrough. I stopped saving stuff just because it marked an event or experience, and began saving stuff that delivered the essence and stories of each theme.

Since then I've explored several themes and many stories. Themes led to stories and stories led to themes. To be clear, this was not a step-by-step, clear-cut linear process. Random. Fluid. Jagged. Meandering. Off-track. New track. These are more accurate descriptors of this multi-month process that is never completely done until we are. But my goal is to claim and hold up the best stories and lessons from my life for myself and, down the road, for others.

So I went with the flow, to a point. When a story took me deep down memory lane I followed, observing my response and listening for a core theme that felt like part of my legacy. When my list of core themes grew too long I sorted out lesser themes. Often those themes described a means by which I lived out a bigger theme.

For example "embrace life" and "travel" were both on my first theme list. But "embrace life" is the bigger theme. "Travel" is one of several ways in which I embrace life. So, "embrace life" remains a core theme under which I highlight my travel stories.

Likewise a single theme can be the foundation for a wide variety of stories. For example, under my family theme there are stories about fun, kindness, love, persistence, respect, openness, acceptance, and support through good times and bad. One theme. Many storylines that all point to the same theme.

When I felt anxious, bad or stuck in old negative places I moved on. Some days I dug through stuff. Some days I ignored it all and rode my bike. And some days I stood back and surveyed my space and my stuff: a specific room (kitchen), one set of stuff (books), one item (heirloom vase), or simply did a mental scan of everything. Then I'd consider the themes, personal values or characteristics reflected in the space and stuff (e.g., family, perseverance, music, adventure, wellness).

Here are a few questions that helped me hone in on the keepers. I hope a few of these lead you to discover your own.

- *Does this story showcase a core theme of my life?*
- *Are there stories that more clearly reflect this theme?*
- *Is this story (or set of stories) part of a larger theme?*

All of it was food for thought. Every thought helped me rediscover what mattered to me. For decades I could barely keep up with the responsibilities of daily life. It felt great to rediscover stories from my life that reflected a legacy I'd be proud to leave.

Today my legacy stories fall within five roughly defined themes: family, music, embracing life, finding a way, creating a welcoming environment.

These may change as I live out the rest of my life, but for now if loved ones can see and feel these five themes reflected in my stuff–whether or not they use these terms–I'll have left them something of value.

LESSONS LEARNED

Six useful lessons also emerged about selecting stories:

1. *Not all good stories are important in the long run*

Not every item needs to be kept and not every story needs to be passed on. Nor does its stuff need to be housed with us until the end. Moving out stuff from old stories (or someone else's stories) frees up physical and emotional space to enjoy the stories that enrich life today.

Some stories were important in the past but in the grand scheme of our lives play a supporting role. For example, my first eighteen years were about theatre and music. At the age of nineteen I turned my attention completely to music and left theatre behind. But, I kept every script, every program and photo from those years. Do these tell a legacy story? No. A side, fun story, yes, but not a legacy story. It would be sad if these stories distracted from bigger stories I want my loved ones to take with them. So, I donated my playbooks, put a couple programs in a photo album and ditched the rest.

Some stories are just about today. Helping my elderly mother is a top priority that takes much of my time right now. While I hope to be remembered as someone who stepped up in time of need, it is more important to me that my loved ones remember other stories from our time together (and their own time spent with Grandma) than that they remember stories of me caring for her.

2. *Tough stories require care*

Life includes stories of tough times. Divorce, unemployment, health crises, family struggles, legal issues, loss of a home (or homeland), and for some, violence.

As I come across remnants from my own tough times (often in writings or photos) I pause and ask myself what, if anything, from this experience is important to preserve. The same goes for long buried family secrets.

The goal isn't to forget or downplay tough times but to act with sensitivity toward loved ones who may not have thought about these events for some time. Once I'm gone they'll no longer have the benefit of discussion.

If surviving a tough time is a key legacy story, look for items that highlight the values or learnings from this experience such as marks of strength, hope and perseverance. Share the story with loved ones now or consider writing a personal summary to leave with a photo or other artifact. Otherwise, let it go.

3. Cherished items hold clues to cherished stories

We rarely cherish an item for its market value. But we do cherish an item for the emotions it evokes; the stories, experiences and people it reconnects us to.

For example, I have a rare copy (albeit not monetarily valuable) of the 1966 Hullabaloo Dance Book. With absolutely no hesitation I can fully describe why I cannot let go of this silly little book: (a) it is pure fun, (b) it takes up so little room it's a surprise every time I come across it, (c) it's an instruction manual with photos; in essence, everything you need (besides crepe paper and LPs) to host a REAL 60's sock hop, and (d) it makes people laugh. I don't care if the kids keep it. I just want them to see it as they sort through my stuff because it will make them laugh.

In contrast I have a 1950s silver candelabra from my grandmother that is gorgeous. I received it around the same time I got the Hullabaloo book but for the life of me I can't tell you why I still have it other than it came from Grandma and it is "very nice." I SHOULD love it. I appreciate the original sentiment of the gift. And, I've lugged it around for decades, protected it, polished it. Yet its only place in my story is that it's a box marked "fragile" I continue to move and store. Its story–and it has one that I'll spare you–is attached to others. And that story is completely irrelevant to me and those who come after me.

When the kids see the Hullabaloo book I imagine they'll remember dancing in our living room with holiday blinky lights dangling from the ceiling and the rug actually rolled up –sometimes just family, sometimes one kid with friends, sometimes solo. I hope those memories will spur memories of other fun, wacky stuff our family did. We didn't have money but our house was a welcoming, go-to house for friends. This is a legacy story I want them to take from their childhood.

On the other hand, I imagine them looking at the candelabra and asking "Is this Mom's?"

By all rational measures the candelabra would be considered a cherished item and the Hullabaloo Dance Book not so much. But there is no question which is the cherished item *to me*– cherished as a prop to launch great stories and good feelings I hope loved ones carry with them long after I'm gone.

4. *Cherished stories hold clues to our big themes*

When asked how we want to be remembered, many of us start with a standard list of "good person" qualities: kind, caring, courageous, good provider, and so forth. When I do that, however, I get stuck on the term. Am I really kind? Why do I think so? Do others think of me as kind? And how does kindness connect with my stuff?

I ditched the list and began with cherished stories. Common themes quickly appeared. One batch of stories was about adventure and joy (the Hullabaloo Dance Book falls here). Another batch was about love among family and friends, another about persistence through tough times, and another about being a welcoming environment to others. This is how I want to be remembered. Suddenly it was easy to connect certain stuff with each story.

5. *Some stuff is simply important*

Some stuff is simply important, period. For now. We might not have a direct connection to the item but we know there was a story once, and it feels important to preserve the item for the next generation. Their stories are fairly impersonal and brief: This is a necklace made from a Great Aunt's wedding ring. This is a 100-year old Bible inscribed by an ancestor.

I've placed these items together in a small marked box that will not distract from my stories. The kids might take one look and ditch it all; or an item or two might have some unexpected meaning to someone. At that point it's their decision.

6.   *This is my stuff now, and my stories*

The final and most important lesson for me was that everything living in my space today is my stuff. I am the boss—whether I chose it, inherited it, or it mysteriously appeared in my home. I decide what stuff and stories to highlight and what stuff and stories to move out. I choose to look at things for what they are to me, rather than what they were to someone in the past or might be to someone down the road.

As boss, I decided to offer a select set of items to relatives and friends who had a connection to the item. Examples included items from family history, special artwork, and quirky fun stuff. And as boss, I established and shared a time-bound, three-step process:

Ask. Confirm. Believe.

Ask: "Do you want this? Please let me know by Thursday."

> If there was no response by Thursday, I checked in.

> If their response was "Yes I'd like this item", we discussed delivery.

> If the response was "Maybe", I gave them a couple more days to make a decision.

If their response was "No", I confirmed their decision:

Confirm: "Are you sure?"

> If their response was "I think so..." we talked. Sometimes I agreed to hold the item for a specific period of time, such as when someone was in the process of moving. More often, the conversation felt like part of their own process of letting go. Many conversations were touching; moments of remembrance and care.

> If their response was "I'm sure I don't want this." I moved on to step three:

Believe: "Thanks. I'll move forward with other plans for this item." And then I did.

> There were no second guesses. ("She says no, but I'm sure she'll want this later.") There were no "backsies." New owners were new *owners.* I held a firm "no return" policy.

Today, I know my themes will survive without keeping each and every relevant item. In fact, my themes come to life when I choose and highlight the best stuff–stuff that prompts legacy stories.

TELLING A BIG STORY IN A SHORT TIME

With my core themes coming together, legacy stories were taking shape. So, how could I preserve them? I didn't plan to write out the stories. Nor would there be a tour guide to add colorful narrative as the kids boxed up my things ("and on your left...") The stuff and stories would have to speak for themselves and still merge seamlessly into my current life.

And no matter how big the story, it had to be concisely conveyed. Leaving eighteen boxes of stuff related to a lifelong hobby would not cut it. Leaving one box of well-chosen items that highlight why this was a lifelong hobby would.

How could I draw attention to stories that pointed to themes, not as essays or professional exhibits, but within an environment I called home? When friends and family walk into my place, what themes appear? What stories emerge with a closer look? I needed expert insight.

Again I leapt outside the box. Why not? It had become a comfortable place to be. Who creates space to tell a story that brings people to life? Whose job is it to tell a clear, succinct and compelling story as quickly as possible incorporating stuff? Where had I see this done well? Who are the experts?

Interior designers, feng shui experts, and home staging professionals create mood and order. But I wanted my place to shout "family", "musician", "fun"; in a quiet, practical, obvious way. There would be no banners, no poster boards. This was not marketing; this was my home.

The experts I needed were waiting behind the curtain–of theatre, television, and film.

Every show, every episode, every storyline must be told quickly, clearly, and succinctly, using physical things to set a scene. When I enter a high school gym for a production of "Grease" the stage sets an upbeat, fun, toe-tapping mood before the overture begins. When I turn on the TV I know if the show is a sitcom, drama or documentary before a word is spoken. I'm either drawn in or turn the channel in roughly five seconds. Clear, succinct, compelling (or not).

Next there's the efficiency of scriptwriting. What a talent it is to write three or four storylines that include character development and plotlines for roughly 22 minutes of screen time. Thinking about scriptwriting led to a larger exploration of how to craft a clear, succinct, compelling story. I sought wisdom from professional bloggers, scriptwriters, columnists, storyboard artists, and a poet.

What I found was enlightening, useful, and immensely fun to ponder.

A handful of tips popped up over and over:

- Start with an image.
- Keep it brief and simple.
- Don't feel you have to explain everything.
- Stories can be about very small stuff so long as the emotions are big.
- Stories are about how you felt about what transpired; less about winning, more about how you felt when you won (or didn't).

But my favorite storytelling tips came from the masters at Pixar; creators of "Toy Story", "Up", "Finding Nemo", "Inside Out", and "Coco" to name a few.[3] The titles alone bring to mind compelling characters and nuanced storylines.

Here are a handful of Pixar storytelling rules (paraphrased) that I immediately put to use:
- What's the essence of your story? The most economical telling of it?
- Characters are admired for trying more than success.

---

[3] "The 22 rules of storytelling, according to Pixar" by Cyriaque Lamar, compiled by Pixar storyboard artist Emma Coats

- Give us a reason to root for the character.
- Simplify. You'll feel like you're losing valuable stuff but it sets you free.
- Let go even if it's not perfect. Know the difference between doing your best and fussing.
- Pull apart the stories you like. What you like in them is a part of you

Here's how I translated these tips for my task:

Start with an image: Standing at my front door looking in, what mood is set? What message? This is your starting image.

Keep it brief and simple: When the first image is clean, uncluttered and somewhat orderly (we do live here after all), there is a sense of peace and calm–that the important things are present and can be found.

Let go even if it's not perfect. Know the difference between doing your best and fussing: There will always be a bit of clutter, a coat to donate, or an item in the wrong room.

The goal is not perfection. The goal is living fully the life you want today, preserving the stories you most hope to leave behind, and, in the process, avoiding a messy cleanup for loved ones. Balance actions carefully among these goals, never forgetting to live your life while you strive to achieve the other two goals.

As I reflected on my themes and the legacy stories I most wanted to preserve, I thought about the essence of each story. What were the essential elements of this story? How could it be told simply yet fully? What image or item might spark a loved one's memory of the story?

CHOOSING STUFF TO CONVEY A STORY

Again, I paused. Where I had seen this done well? Whose legacy stories were alive in their space, intermingled with, but not intruding on, their daily life? Whose stuff didn't feel like stuff but felt like stories? My favorite uncle's home came to mind.

Uncle Rich was a figure skater. He always had a day job but skating defined his life. Uncle Rich (Dick Day to the skating world) was full of stories from learning to skate on a farm pond to judging figures for future Olympians. When he died he left select figurines, artwork, photos, programs, and yes, skates.

While he was alive these items adorned his tastefully decorated, lemon-scented home. There were also tidy stashes of magazines, neatly stacked boxes in the garage, and other signs of daily life. Nothing that distracted from his core legacy story: live your dream. When he died his nieces and nephews each took one item that brought to mind stories of the uncle they knew and loved.

Uncle Rich's home conveyed the theme that meant the most to him: his life in skating. His possessions and the care he took to present them told story upon story, bringing this theme–and him–to life. And, his home was a comfortable, practical, clearly lived-in space. I wanted to be like my uncle. How did he decide which stuff, nice as it might be, was redundant or a distraction?

Which professionals know how to mix scene and story with a practical, fluid result?

First, I returned to lessons from the stage and read about award-winning scene design.

And I met with my friend Judi who has spent a lifetime in the theatre. My questions to her: "How does a set designer choose items to shape a story? What sets a good scene?"

Judi began with a story of her own. "After a particularly good performance a few of us went backstage to congratulate the actors and crew. A friend approached the set designer, shook his hand and said, 'The set design was exceptional. I don't remember a thing about it after the play began.'" The point: every item in the set was so well integrated with the play that it kept this viewer's focus on the characters and their storyline. It facilitated the story but didn't distract.

"The best items are at first obvious and then merge into the scene." she continued. "They set a mood and connect the audience to the characters. How do you want the audience to feel? What do you want them to expect? Where do you want them to look? Different people will notice different things, but the mood elicited should be consistent. Once the action begins, these items blend into the background."

Her words described Uncle Rich's home to a T. We were definitely on to something.

Reflecting on her response I imagined various items in my home setting a mood or connecting to those who enter. I want people to feel welcomed, to expect calm and comfort. I want them to notice family pictures and music. Not specifics, just that family and music reflect who I am and what I value. I want stuff to highlight these stories, blended within the framework of daily life.

Next, I spoke with a friend who recently retired from a lifelong career with a large history museum. When I mentioned selecting possessions to bring our stories to life, she suggested this was akin to being curators of our own collections.

She explained that museum curators don't simply choose nice things to put on display. Curators are trained to select and display objects that, together, best tell the story to be portrayed. Top curators are experts at "reading" an object. What makes this item special (among dozens)? How does this object complement or distract from other items that relate to the main story? Will viewers be able to emotionally connect with the object? Might it prompt their own memories and stories?

This was exactly what I wanted to do: identify, preserve, and highlight items that, together, would tell my legacy stories and themes while prompting loved ones' own stories. And, while integrating these items and stories with daily life in my home.

Finally I spoke with a third friend who is a master at creating simple, practical spaces that reflect the lives of the people who live there. We met when I sold my last house. After months on the market I'd moved and was eager to sell. A new realtor suggested Sharon's services. As the realtor said, "Sharon just has an eye."

When I entered my house I felt as if I knew (and liked) the phantom family who lived there. Each room contained typical items found in a bedroom, den, living room, office, but without clutter, without distractors. Stagers do this. I tried to do this. But Sharon had reached a deeper level. The stuff Sharon selected didn't just convey a room's function; it also told you who these people were. Sharon brought their (albeit imaginary) stories to life.

At the open house prospective buyers connected with the imaginary owners. "Where does your son play ball?" "Do you work from home, too?" The house sold in two days. I asked Sharon to help me set up my new place. My home environment has never been more practical, more comfortable, and more me. Sharon has more than an eye; she also has heart.

Today Sharon is also a senior move manager. Every day she helps clients create an environment that supports current interests and needs (and realities), without losing the stories they loved.

To begin, Sharon talks with the client about setting the scene for a given area. How does the resident use the space? Feel comfortable? What fits and what's out of place—in this space, for this person, at this time? She seeks first to understand who the individual is and what is important to him or her for the long run as well as in daily life. Then she helps them choose stuff to highlight their best stories and meet their practical needs.

For example, Roy has 100 sports bobble head figurines. Ninety-seven of the bobble heads may or may not have street value (remember Beanie Babies?) Three tell a legacy story. There's the first one Roy received—a birthday gift from 7-year old grandson Sammy with whom he played catch. Then there's the one Roy and Sammy got at Sammy's first major league game for being among the first thousand fans to arrive that day. The third Sam sent to Roy when Sammy's college team, also Roy's alma mater, won their division championship.

Those three bobble heads hold a legacy story. Roy's other 97 may hold mini stories, but are likely to distract from the major legacy story of Roy and Sammy. Roy kept those three; and Sam has requested them when the time comes.

As expected, Sharon offered a few basics:

- Keep it simple and clean
- Blend special things with your life today
- Space and collections should be easy to maintain (and change for any reason or just because you want to)

When you succeed:

- The space feels calm with few distractions
- The space reflects who you are today
- Things don't take up space you really want for something else

Both Judi and Sharon also suggest hiding fun "aha" moments in plain sight like little gems to be discovered. It can be whatever you want. I did this with a small set of fun books: The Hullabaloo Dance Book, Outhouses of Alaska, Claw Your Way to the Top (a Dave Barry classic)… my goal being to simply offer a touch of comic relief during an otherwise dreary task through our family's appreciation for humor.

Armed with lessons from the experts, it was time to pull it all together.

The next chapter describes how I tackled ten categories of stuff to preserve my stories, embrace today, and avoid leaving a mess–and how you might, too.

PART II

Welcome to Part II!

Part II is the hands-on part of the book where you'll tie your themes and legacy stories to your stuff. This is an ongoing process, not a once-and-done event. Why? Because you are still alive and living your life. New stuff comes in, interests change, stories happen. And that's a good thing.

Chapter 4 walks you through ten categories in which our stuff lives (photos, furniture, clothes and so forth). Each section describes stories and challenges typically found in a category, how I tackled the category, and tips if you get stuck.

Categories are presented in no particular order. Start anywhere. Skip around. Ignore any category that isn't a fit for you. I've included a blank template at the end to add your own category if you wish.

Chapter 5 offers a glimpse into life today among my best stories, a few fun resources, and final words.

Part II ends with an epilogue; a fictional story of a little girl named Esther and how her stuff grew, and grew, and grew…until today.

Take what's useful. Skip over the rest. This is your life, your stories. Do whatever helps to:

- Preserve and highlight themes and stories you want loved ones to remember
- Prevent a messy cleanup
- Free up your time, space and energy for today

Chapter Four

PUTTING IT ALL TOGETHER

"The ability to simplify means to eliminate the unnecessary
so that the necessary may speak."
Hans Hoffman

If you're a detail person like me, you may have a few final
questions.

- What stuff is fair game?
- Are there ground rules?
- Tips to get started or stay on track?
- Why not just start in the attic and work down (and
  out…to the garage, the storage shed, the cabin, and so
  forth)?

This is how I answered those questions.

STUFF THAT'S FAIR GAME

"Stuff" includes all physical items and e-stuff owned (by
choice or chance) or stored for someone else because (a) it is
your responsibility today whether it is used or stored and (b)
someone will have to eventually deal with it (find, donate,
ditch, keep, sell). In other words, everything, every *thing,* is
fair game. Sure there are some rules we'll discuss in the next
section. But being all-inclusive means you can start anywhere,
shift gears and still be on track. No step is too small. Even
cleaning a shelf in the refrigerator counts.

There's stuff we want for now but rarely use (favorite outfit, piano), stuff we have no feelings toward except that it be present (e.g., the couch, toothpaste), and stuff we don't want (clutter, redundant or outdated stuff).

There are everyday items of life (e.g., clothes, kitchenware, wall art, tools, car). There are things tied to personal interests or hobbies (past or present). There are things tied to work (past or present). And there are things that were gifts, memorabilia, items of value (personal, actual, or imagined), collections, heirlooms, electronic stuff, and stuff that qualifies as trash.

Some of us have stuff we store for others. There is stuff we agreed to store "temporarily" during, say, a friend's divorce or while a child "got on his feet." If years have passed and their stuff remains, decide how much longer you want to keep it. Share your decision, be reasonable, and then move it along.

In contrast, if you signed a contract that allows Fred and Ethel to store their accumulated possessions in your garage, you're stuck with it until the contract ends. Likewise if you offered to temporarily store possessions for a friend who's on duty in the military, or for a neighbor whose roof blew off in a tornado, honor the agreement.

Finally, as my friend Sharon says, "Keeping everything distinguishes nothing." Given the Discovery Half-Day as a guideline for human attention, energy, and availability, our best stuff and stories have to be obvious to shine.

To make them obvious become the curator for exhibits about you. Select a few items that best tell your themes and stories. Let go of the extras that might distract. (Remember the bobble head story in Part I? Keep the three that shape the story.)

GROUND RULES

- ***You are the boss*** Absent prior agreements (to store, to offer, to discuss) you have the power to decide stuff's fate right now. Engaging others is a choice.

- ***No guilt, no judgment*** Keep, ditch or skip over anything for any reason.

- ***Go at your own pace*** Pause, stop or switch gears at any point. Take a walk. Go to France.

- ***Find moments for fun and reflection*** Both are essential.

- ***Keep your goals front and center*** Preserve legacy stories. Prevent a messy cleanup. Make room for today.

QUICK STARTS

When you get stuck or don't know where to begin, start with one of these:

Put like things together

For a quick win put like things together, even if it is just re-shelving books or pulling odd stuff out of a junk drawer. Those who religiously follow this well-worn mantra save loved ones countless hours wondering where to look for important documents (or tools, or photos, and so forth). It also saves us time and money looking for (and repurchasing) misplaced items.

Give most, sell some

This mantra along with heartwarming donation stories remind me to avoid chasing pennies. It is amazing how often an item is exactly what someone needs once I let it go.

Here are my thoughts on garage sales, selling stuff online, and so forth. If this is a fun hobby or if an item is likely to bring $100 or more or the money is earmarked for something, go forth and sell. But, consider: you could be done already.

Donating the stuff now recaptures the time and energy it takes to price it, set up tables, manage an online sale, sit in the heat or rain, deal with bargain hunters, etc. Imagine the happy face of a homeless vet finding a winter coat in just his size, or a second grader discovering a "twirly" dress–her first–the day before her school concert; both true stories. Or consider this:

Donating versus selling is like winning a contest where the prize is time ☺

Minimize decisions (and questions)

Decisions take energy. One of the kindest things we can do for loved ones is minimize the decisions they'll have to make about our stuff. The bigger the mess the greater the chance loved ones will be compelled to make a blanket decision to toss it all–or hire someone to do just that; both are emotional and expensive decisions to leave behind.

Many decisions include preliminary decisions and implementation steps. Before you can sell the car you need the title, and the insurance info, and so forth. The more we can simplify and eliminate, the easier their life (and ours) will be.

Get appraisals. Put important documents together. Minimize the steps required to reach and implement a decision. In the process you'll also minimize the number of stuff-related decisions on your plate, leaving energy for new decisions. "Should I plan a trip or read a book today?"

Mark important information on each item that has a particular meaning. A STABILO All pencil works on just about anything–photos, china, glass, metal, plastic, stone. Pencils cost about a buck and change, and are available online and at art stores. Plus, they come in a bunch of fun colors.

If you have a pet, have a plan in place for their care. This is not a decision you want to place on grieving loved ones. Allergies, finances, renting restrictions, lifestyle, or personal choice may limit Fido or Fluffy's relocation options. Make tentative arrangements for your pet's care now. Then make it easy for loved ones to carry out those plans.

Keep your pet's medical, microchip and pet insurance records in an easy-to-find folder. Post your veterinarian's business card on the fridge. Consider allocating a pet care fund in your will, or at least a note in your checkbook with sufficient funds for a few months of kibble. Pets feel like family for many of us; and many pets grieve. Having a plan in place is a good idea no matter what stage in life you are.

To summarize, make decisions now about stuff that doesn't matter to loved ones. Consider pre-gifting items designated in a will; discuss the story and why it is being gifted now. If you get stuck simply ask yourself: How can I minimize decisions?

LOCATIONS OR CATEGORIES?

Locations

In literal terms a location is a place. For our purposes–to preserve stories and minimize cleanup–locations are places where miscellaneous stuff gets stored. Prime examples include the attic, basement, garage, closets, that "extra" room, off-site storage, cabin, and (yes) e-storage. Locations are named on to-do lists and in aspirational promises such as "Saturday I'm going to clean the basement."

When we're in our prime years, the good news is locations tend to hold a lot of random stuff; stuff like Grandpa's old set of golf clubs earmarked for Billie (who's 2), the six-foot candy cane used in an annual neighborhood display, and the barbells from college that we plan to use to get back in shape.

As we think about preserving stories and minimizing cleanup decisions, the bad news is that locations tend to hold a lot of the same random stuff; victims of the directive, "I'll just put in the attic for now." And for the record, Billie is now 27 and never played golf; the candy cane display was discontinued in 1987, and the barbells…well they must be somewhere.

When the goal is decluttering, tackling a location works well. Progress is visible. Lost items are discovered. There is a braggable sense of accomplishment. ("I cleaned out the attic!") But it is also easy to get overwhelmed by the volume and variety of stuff let alone knowing where to put it all.

Categories

In contrast, categories *provide an initial gathering scheme and place* around which to bring like things together. This makes it easier to answer questions such as:

- Is there a special item of art (or jewelry, or a mixing bowl, or screwdriver) I want to highlight in a legacy story?
- Which items in this category are part of my life today – or that I want to keep just because?

- What can I do today to facilitate and minimize decisions for the final disposition of stuff in *this category*?

Categories also **connect personal themes and stories**. Our major life themes tend to leave a trail of connecting stories and items from multiple categories. Remember Aunt Betty from Chapter 3? Entertaining (with an emphasis on cooking) was a major theme kept alive through stories loved ones experienced with Aunt Betty. Items that prompt those memories come from various categories: her special serving plate (kitchen), holiday table cloths (linens), published recipes (books), snapshots from gatherings (photos). Highlighting objects from various categories gives depth to the importance of this theme in Aunt Betty's life.

Categories also make it easy to **distinguish story-rich personal stuff from stuff that is primarily utilitarian or simply reflects lifestyle.** Personal stuff holds memories and emotions. This is the stuff we hope loved ones notice; stuff we'd hate to see get accidentally tossed. On the opposite end, utilitarian stuff typically requires few decisions (e.g., this is all give away, everything goes to Billy's for his first apartment). Most categories include a mix of personal, lifestyle and utilitarian stuff, but some may not.

For example, my kitchen is completely utilitarian. Other than a couple heirloom pieces stored in a cabinet, bandits could come in after I'm gone, steal every last spoon and crumb, and nothing important would be lost (in fact that would really save some time...) Thus I approached this category as a great opportunity to save loved ones' time for story-rich categories. I cleared out the last of the items I no longer use, put like things together, did a once-through for random crumbs, and moved on. The best part is how quickly I can find things now.

As you read through the next section keep in mind these are categories and examples that worked for me–so far. My stuff, my stories, my subjective categories. You may want to do less, do more, or do something entirely different to preserve your stories and minimize cleanup decisions for your loved ones.

Three of the ten categories are not typically thought of as "stuff": e-stuff, money and important documents, and residential and non-residential property. Yet, without a little forethought, these categories can cause significant stress and distract loved ones from the affirming stories we hope to leave behind. The good news is that there are ample ways to minimize and simplify decisions. Your loved ones will thank you in absentia.

FOOD FOR THOUGHT

Food for thought: My museum friend introduced me to the concept of an objects collections policy. This is an official statement used by collection specialists to guide their decisions about obtaining new items – and "deaccessioning" objects currently in the collection. Although I do not foresee a policy manual in my future, I love the idea of a guideline for allowing new stuff in, such as "from now on I'll only buy things I will wear, need or use now–no matter how good a bargain it is." Plus the thought of "deaccessioning" possessions feels far less judgmental than say, "decluttering."

Likewise, consider having a conversation with friends or family about gifts. Perhaps you've been collecting butterfly pins for years but are ready to be done. Maybe there is a family tradition of gift giving that has become more about the tradition than the exchange.

Consider exchanging gifts of experiences or time (trip to the zoo, baseball game, tuition to a community education course or dance classes, or a coupon for babysitting for overworked parents–complete with movie tickets). Other non-stuff ideas are gifts of food, flowers, or a donation in someone's honor. If you buy gifts for a family with kids, consider a family membership to a children's museum, a summer water park, or something similar that boosts time with family and friends.

And now for my favorite donation story. When my oldest grandsons were in grade school their uncle gave them a small but meaningful tangible holiday gift. He also gave $50 to donate to help someone or something else.

He scheduled time with them and brought information on three pre-selected charities (approved by the parents). He and the boys talked about what each charity did, how the money was used, and who was helped. Once a charity was chosen, Uncle Tony helped them complete the donation form and send in the contribution. Many lessons were learned in the process.

As you make discoveries along the way, your themes, stories and categories may change. Have fun. Do a little here, a little there. Make this your own.

So now, on to the ten categories.

CATEGORIES

Presented in no particular order.

Start anywhere.

Move around.

PHOTOS

The Stories Photos Leave Behind

Photos visually preserve our life stories for future generations. As such they provide important links to our themes.

Photos fall into three categories:

1. Print photos of life events (mostly taken by us)
2. Print photos inherited from past generations
3. Digital

Family photography was a luxury for our grandparents, a middle class symbol for our parents, and an assumption for us (who else had a Brownie?) When our grandparents or great-grandparents sailed to America they left family behind, possibly for good. Travel options were unavailable or financially inaccessible, thus the relatively new technology of photography was precious. Today email, texting, Facetime, and travel options make it easy to stay in touch.

Consequently, family photos were treasured and passed down from generation to generation, even after the identity of the people or place was long forgotten. If you have boxes of loose photos and photo albums, including crumbling albums from past generations, you are not alone.

Some of us also have many little boxes (or big carousels) of carefully preserved slides or countless envelopes of negatives. I saved a few gems from the slides, tossed the negatives and focused on what, to me, were actual photos (digital and print). That was plenty!

At the broadest level what are the stories you hope your photo collection will leave behind?

Discovery Half-Day & Photos

Nowhere is the Discovery Half-Day challenged more than with photos. The emotional tug of photos is strong and time-consuming. Hours can fly by with little progress. The challenge is compounded when there are generations' worth of disorganized print photos.

In order to save our entire photographic family history from the dumpster, we must reduce the overall volume and then highlight photos that tell the stories we want to preserve. Start with whatever makes sense to you. As you sift through photos:

1. Look for photos that highlight a theme or key story.
2. Put those photos together.
3. Keep reducing until you have a reasonable number.
4. Eliminate the rest.

How I Tackled Photos

As you know, family is one of my themes. Besides inherited photos, most of my photos are family birthdays, graduations, holidays, trips, and a whole slew of just-because-you're-here photos (which I believe is in the Grandmother's creed...but I digress). The rest are of friends who I consider family.

In the end, the story I want my photos to send loved ones and generations to come is simply this: *You matter.* Period. You matter to me as my child, my grandchild, my friend. That's where I began.

Print Photos

To begin I put "like things together." This was not a fast or perfect process but it got me started. Sorting through print-based photos of my own life events was fairly easy because I started at a really high level. Good photos were kept; marginal photos tossed. When possible I grouped themes, similar events or at least photos of similar people in piles, shoeboxes or zip lock bags. Extra copies of good photos were offered to family. It was awhile before I was ready for albums.

This was a stop-and-go process that–I'm not kidding–took a couple years to get my arms around. Sorting through photos could easily send me down memory lane, at times dredging up difficult emotions and zapping energy. I needed to take it slow with lots of breaks. But I eventually got there.

Sorting through inherited photos presented a different set of challenges. In contrast to easily replicated digital photos, tossing any of these faded, last-copy photos felt like tossing relatives to the wind. Eventually I realized most of our family photos from yesteryear are best described as "old guy with a fish" or "bunch of people I don't know in an unknown place and time." Few have clues that might connect them to me.

Rather than pass this mystery along to another generation, I decided to organize my print-based photos into clearly marked albums that are accessible right now. These will be simple to divide up when the time comes. Again, I gave family members a couple chances to take extra photos that didn't make the albums. Remaining photos were tossed. The resulting albums are easy to maintain:

- Adult child's name (1-2 albums each)
- Grandchildren by family unit (1-2 albums each)
- Mixed photos of immediate family (1 album)
- Legacy albums of each set of grandparents & their ancestors (1 album each)
- Legacy album from my childhood (1 album)
- Legacy album of my music career (1 album)

- Current personal memories album of special events, solo trips, visits to friends (1 album)

Occasionally I take an hour or so to update the albums with recent photos.

Digital Photos

Digital photos have revolutionized how we view, share and save pictures. I wanted a quick fix to ensure the pictures that didn't make it into an album weren't lost–yep, just in case.

The best solution for me was a flash-drive based photo management program. A few times a year I plug in the flash drive, click "start" and it downloads ALL the photos from my laptop, no matter where they are squirreled away. The flash drive is clearly marked and kept with the keys to my fire safe for easy discovery. The flash drive may or may not work with future software, but for now I know my digital photos are in one place and can be found. It isn't a perfect solution but it gives me peace.

The Payoff

- New photos are easy to add as the family expands or trips are taken. There is no more stress over picture projects. And no more boxes of random photos!

- The albums facilitate conversations about family history, traditions, and meaningful events. Even my teen and toddler grandchildren regularly pull out an album or two. "That's me!"

- Photos prompt theme stories: music performances, travel to Chile, quirky birthday cakes made for family gatherings. And, when the time comes, the first thing loved ones will see upon entering my home is the set of albums that display their names, a reminder of love as they begin the emotionally-charged process of sorting through my stuff.

- And should a health crisis land me in a care facility, loved ones can easily grab favorite photos to brighten the smaller space.

Tips if You Get Stuck

- Gather all your print photos and host a two-hour family photo-sorting event. Play old family videos or childhood music in the background. Toss any unclaimed photos. Eat afterwards.

- Create a thumb drive of favorite family photos for each child or grandchild. My cousin did one of these for me.

- Use an online service to create a book of special stories with photos for each loved one (especially young grandkids). Leave one page for them to add their memories of you.

- Take a break.

- Too many trip photos? Eliminate duplicate or similar photos and bad ones (dark, fuzzy, head cut-off). Group the remaining photos by event or scenery. Pull out the least engaging photos in each group; repeat. The final photos should tell the story you want them to know or remember.

- Historically-relevant photos? While most history centers are flooded with old photos, if you have something truly unique or noteworthy ask your local history center to suggest possible donation sites.

Does My Photo Collection Tell the Story I Want to Leave Behind? *Use this section to jot down items that highlight a legacy story or to note special items you intend to pass down. Are the items easy to find? Marked, organized? Note any special care required to preserve, showcase or pass down an item. Or use this space to doodle.*

FURNITURE

The Stories Furniture Leaves Behind

Furniture conveys how we use our space. This is an office. An art studio. A cozy den. A guest bedroom for the grandkids. Furniture sets the scene where stories unfold in our home. Most of our furniture is a backdrop for our personality, lifestyle, and interests. A few items may carry legacy stories.

Take the old sitcom, "Frasier." When Frasier's dad, Martin, moves in he brings his chair–an old, ugly recliner complete with duct tape; an item that remains center stage for all eleven seasons. In one particularly touching episode Martin describes the life stories connected to that chair. For him, this chair represents and keeps special memories (and people) alive; an homage to the importance of family to this crusty old guy. In contrast the entire rest of the set conveys the personality, lifestyle and interests of Frasier; in a much less intimate way.

Like Martin, we may have a favorite piece of furniture that holds our important life or legacy stories. If so, share the stories now. The rest is probably backdrop.

The Discovery Half-Day & Furniture

For many of us, loved ones' *decisions* about furniture won't be a big problem as most furniture will likely be donated. Even sentimental items like Martin's chair may go.

Realistically, few millennials want our old furniture. It doesn't fit with their space or style. Plus furniture can be a challenge to move. Buying online means it shows up at their door. And they feel differently about "but it's free" than we do.

If you have antiques, designer pieces with significant value, or particularly quirky or deeply sentimental items, now is the time to:

- Distinguish these from everything else.
- Get appraisals, find certificates of authentication etc.
- Clarify if a loved one wants a specific item; gift it now or note it in a will.

Do any items highlight or facilitate an important theme or personal story? Perhaps the sleeper sofa makes it possible to host grandkids or maybe the funky bookcase reminds you of Aunt Josie who taught you how to read. Keep those. Then decide which items serve your current lifestyle or you simply want to keep. For example, everything on my desk stays. Two items relate to themes and I currently use everything else.

Finally, distribute the rest. You'll have the furniture you use and want, and you'll minimize family conflict and hassle down the road.

How I Tackled Furniture

A few years back I sold a four-bedroom home with finished basement, two car garage and a fairytale playhouse–and moved to a one-bedroom condo with a six-by-eight foot storage locker. That meant a lot of furniture had to go. My furniture fell into two broad categories: (a) currently useful and/or especially loved, or (b) formerly-useful pieces from the past. The more I donated (before and after the move), the more space I had to play with.

Sometimes the empty space provided much-needed breathing room. Occasionally it called out for something new. Shopping for new items felt like furnishing my first home; like a do-over to design my living space.

By matching my furniture to my current lifestyle and my themes, my whole place felt lighter.

The Payoff

- Your space reflects the lifestyle you are living NOW.

- Calmer space. Better feng shui ☺

- Fewer tripping hazards.

- Items of value are appraised, assigned and marked.

- Fewer things means fewer disagreements over silly stuff once you're gone.

Tips if You Get Stuck

- Have a family-only give-away weekend for good items you no longer use/want.

- Post gently loved unwanted items on a free stuff website. If giving away an old couch feels like a loss, consider the monetary and physical value of not having to move it yourself.

- Send relatives a last-call email (with time limit) for family heirlooms and antiques you are ready to release. Include pictures and brief descriptions.

- Ask yourself "What could go here if I got rid of the [old piece I don't really like, use or want]?" I created a grandkid area that gets regular use and makes me happy just to look at.

- Remember, to older generations, an item might have been a tangible connection to a loved one from the old country. But, to younger generations YOU are that loved one. And you are right here. They care about *you*–not your stuff. That's how you raised them (or their parents). Let the item go and call someone special.

Does My Furniture Tell the Story I Want to Leave Behind? *Use this section to jot down items that highlight a legacy story or to note special items you intend to pass down. Are the items easy to find? Marked, organized? Note any special care required to preserve, showcase or pass down an item. Or use this space to doodle.*

BOOKS, FILMS AND MUSIC

The Stories Books, Films and Music Leave Behind

Books, films (family and commercial), and music provide clues to our past and current interests. Some items from generations past may reflect family history. Others may be central to a theme, or legacy story.

However, without some organization and care, large collections may simply say "Bill loved books" rather than "Bill loved mystery novels!"

Then there are surprises.

I recently learned that some used bookstores no longer accept children's books printed before 1985 because some were printed with lead-based ink. Who knew? That raises a whole set of questions about the dust I breathed going through bags of childhood books and old home movies. It may be all fine (as long as no one chews on the book), but the message this drives home is that old does not necessarily equal awesome.

Technology has had a tremendous impact on books, films and music. Besides the need to update our personal equipment, these shifts continue to impact the ability to access collections created with obsolete technologies. For example, the bags I inherited of old home movies included five film platforms, each requiring different viewing equipment. Transferring the whole lot to DVD was a commitment of time and money.

In contrast, my grandson has little need to *own* any of these items. He borrows e-books through Amazon Prime, watches movies on Netflix, and listens to the music of his choice through Spotify. If he wants to take a photo or video he uses his smartphone (where, by the way, he can also listen to music, read books or watch films albeit with a small screen). And, by the time you read this he'll be using something even newer. His legacy stories will be preserved through technologies yet to be invented.

What legacy stories are reflected in your books, films and music? How can you preserve them for the next generation?

The Discovery Half-Day & Books, Films and Music

The personal draw of books, films and music can sap hours of sorting and processing time for you and loved ones. Consequently big, undistinguished collections are easy dumpster targets. Plus it takes time and physical energy to pack and deliver heavy boxes (whether to the used book store or Goodwill).

Distinguish the items that mean the most to you from items you simply want to keep for now. For example, I have a CD collection that I understand only has value to me. I like it, use it, and will keep it knowing full well the kids might just ditch it–not because they don't care but because their world is streaming.

While it might be hard to let go of your copy of "Back to the Future", keep in mind that unless an item is irreplaceable (such as home videos), is out-of-print, or has personal significance for you, the library or a streaming service probably has it. And, you can reserve it and maybe read, watch or listen to it online.

How I Tackled Books, Films and Music

I had a lot of books so my first goal was to reduce the number of bookcases in my space. The original goal turned out to be unrealistic but it helped me begin the sorting process. Today I have three bookcases: one for photo albums, one for books and music, one for children's books.

From there my books, films and music fell into five distinct buckets with equally distinct actions:

- **No one wants it:** Ditch commercial VHS tapes, cassettes, tattered and torn books, LPs & CDs that skip or are cracked, sheet music with missing parts/pages (yes, I did that...because I might meet a musician with the missing part/page someday???)

- **It's readily available**: Which of my books, films and music am I *likely* to read or listen to that is *unlikely* to be available at a library or streaming? Save those for now.

- **Personal special collections**:
  - *Keep*: Current or near-term use such as children's books for the grandkids corner and Spanish books because I really DO plan to use them soon.

  - *Maybe keep, maybe not*: Memorabilia such as my high school yearbooks.

  - *Transition*: Someone else's collections that fell in my lap (transition) such as Mom's 1940's LPs. Although the albums are cool to look at, the reality is I'm not a collector, nor do I have a working stereo. Plus they are heavy. A friend framed a few favorite album covers and ditched the warped and cracked records.

- **Special meaning (to keep):**
  - Books that were gifts inscribed with handwritten personal messages.

  - Quality home movies
    - I transferred three generations of home movies to DVDs; roughly 100 tapes that covered 80 years of life translated to 6 hours on DVDs. Not that anyone will watch 6 hours of home movies but we have them, just in case.

- **Items to donate to**:
  - The local library.
  - A neighborhood Little Free Library.
  - Initiatives to collect items for schools in third world countries.

The Payoff

- It's easy to locate the film, book or music you want.

- No more bags of pre-90's "mystery" films.

- Donated books and CDs have a new audience.

- Space is freed up.

- You've save loved ones from the difficult decision to either toss old family videos without knowing what they contain, or take the time to find appropriate viewing equipment and slog through what could be hours of mystery people silently waving.

- You've minimized the schlepping of heavy boxes of books, DVDs, and dare I say...LPs.

- A whittled down collection reminds the sorters of the topics and interests you held most dear.

Tips if You Get Stuck

- Take five. Books, films and music are easy items to tackle in small batches or when thirty minutes (or five) is all you have.

- Let old family films go. Faced with the big, messy, costly task to transfer them to DVD (which itself will be obsolete soon) a lot of families decide to simply ditch old family films. This is a fine option. If you feel compelled, send out one last email to see if anyone wants them. If not, ditch them. No guilt.

- Transfer your CDs to an iPod and donate the rest to the library, an elder care center, day care center, or transitional housing facility.

Do My Books, Films and Music Tell the Story I Want to Leave Behind? *Use this section to jot down items that highlight a legacy story or to note special items you intend to pass down. Are the items easy to find? Marked, organized? Note any special care required to preserve, showcase or pass down an item. Or use this space to doodle.*

KITCHEN

The Stories the Kitchen Leaves Behind

The kitchen is the only category that is also a location. Unlike, say, the attic, most of the stuff in a kitchen is related to the kitchen. Thus I declared "kitchen" a category.

While most of us have stories tied to family meals or celebrations involving food, the stories a kitchen holds vary by how your kitchen is used on a regular basis and whether or not it houses sentimental items. For example, do you come from a line of gourmet chefs and have Grandma Alma's special cake pans or utensils? In some situations, deciding who gets the proverbial "Grandma's cake plate" creates all sorts of conflict.

Likewise, if your kitchen is a gathering place for family, someone might actually want those plastic tiki glasses because of the memories that particular drinkware calls to mind. If those tiki memories are a top priority for how *you* want to be remembered, use them to highlight that story. Otherwise offer the tiki glasses to someone and move on. And for the record, this is a true story–a friend's tiki glasses now reside in my kitchen.

Kitchens may also hold items that were treasured by past generations but few millennials want such as china and actual *silver*ware that must be polished. I have two inherited items I love that I hope become cherished items within the family. Neither requires polishing.

The Discovery Half-Day & the Kitchen

Kitchens offer some great opportunities to minimize decisions, preserve stories, and reduce mess. It takes some work, but both you and your loved ones will reap the benefits.

Tackling a loved one's kitchen can be tedious. Have you ever volunteered to help a friend move and you were assigned to pack up the kitchen? It isn't hard but it can be a real pain. Add the emotion of deciding what to do with Mom's plates–the ones she served your dinner on for 18 years–can bring your energy for decisions to a screeching halt.

For final cleanup purposes your kitchen will likely fall into one of three extremes:

1. Fairly easy to address (keep that platter, toss outdated food, donate the rest)
2. A major packing and cleaning project with emotional memories tied to that space (I remember all our conversations in this room…)
3. Mostly fine but with a few sentimental items that could start a family war.

There are essential items, specialty items, and sentimental items most of which are some combination of bulky, sharp and/or fragile. Many items are heavy and/or bulky, make lots of noise, and are a physical challenge to pack. There are items that have fallen behind cabinets and others stuffed back into a corner. There are drawers of utensils, storage containers, paper products, and of course the junk drawer(s). And crumbs everywhere.

And food. Frozen food, dry food, refrigerated food, food in a separate freezer. A unique set of spices might speak to a cooking-related theme. Outdated canned goods do not.

Finally, if you come from a line of cooks (or perhaps are one yourself), there is a good chance you have a stack of family recipes. Pull them together in one place. Even a gallon-sized zip lock bag is a start. Consider photocopying favorite recipes that are hand-written by relatives long gone. Put the original in a family photo album. Another great option is to create a family recipe book through an online scrapbooking or publishing service. *Gumma's Family Recipes* is an awesome example described in Chapter 5.

Highlight key items related to a theme or legacy story. Keep everything that serves your current needs or you simply like. Then do quick, easy stuff: clean out old food, take everything out of drawers and wipe out the crumbs. Repeat when you get stuck in another category. Give yourself a gold star each and every time.

How I Tackled the Kitchen

My kitchen is small and completely utilitarian; all the action is elsewhere. Nothing happens there to write home about. There are no kitchen stories I wanted to preserve (except, ironically, a DVD titled "Kitchen Stories", a tale of research involving 1950s Norwegian bachelor farmers). Thus, my kitchen was a tremendous place to save loved ones' attention for other stories. From a half-day event perspective, I imagine fifteen minutes or less will be spent on kitchen decisions. Items will go to help families in need, or loved ones will choose random items discovered in the packing phase.

The goal, then, was to make my kitchen the best functional kitchen it could be; for me, for today and the foreseeable future. Even if your kitchen is full of fancy or sentimental cookware or is the center of activity, starting with functionality is a good start.

Here's what I did:

Start with the easy stuff (repeat as needed)

- Throw away outdated food (including spices).
- Toss the rusty pans.
- Ditch the random coffee mugs & dusty plastic cups.
- Toss stained towels and oven mitts with holes.
- Clean out the junk drawer.

What do you really use?

- **Small appliances**
  - Stores are full of attractive small appliances that take up lots of counter or storage space. Given your current (and desired) lifestyle, do you really need a toaster oven *and* a toaster? What about the ice cream maker, the deep fry turkey griller, or the 20-cup coffee maker? Eliminate remnants from the past. Use the counter space for real flowers.

- **Eliminate duplicates**
  - Keep favorites, donate duplicates.

- **Hosting**
  - If you still host large gatherings, by all means keep your service for 20 and the related accoutrements. If the baton has passed to a younger family member, offer the turkey platter to him or her.

  - Save pans to make your special dishes. Share or ditch the rest.

- **Cooking for one or two**
  - o Take a good look at how your cooking and baking habits may differ from twenty years ago. Keep what you use. Pass along the rest.

The Payoff

- You can quickly find whatever you need–including Grandma's special recipes.

- There is more room for art.

- Loved ones won't waste time determining what works and what's broken.

- It will be easy to see and divide what's there: Sue would like that new crockpot, Benny will take the nice salad tongs he gave Mom, and everything else goes to Freedom House.

- Plus, I am still shocked at how much calmer my kitchen feels.

Tips if You Get Stuck

- Pull everything out of the cabinets and put like things together. Kitchen stuff has a tendency to become disorganized. Putting everything in the open helps identify how many pans you have and how many you need.

- Put together starter kitchen sets for young adults who are moving into their first apartment within the next year or donate sets to families in need.

- Donate useable items to senior centers, churches, soup kitchens.

- Gift special items now (e.g., Grandma's cake plate or Grandpa's grill set).

Does My Kitchen Tell the Story I Want to Leave Behind? *Use this section to jot down items that highlight a legacy story or to note special items you intend to pass down. Are the items easy to find? Marked, organized? Note any special care required to preserve, showcase or pass down an item. Or use this space to doodle.*

CLOTHES AND LINENS

The Stories Clothes and Linens Leave Behind

Shirts, pants, dresses, suits, coats, mittens, biking clothes, work shoes, tap shoes, towels, sheets, curtains, hot mitts; if it is fabric or wearable it falls into this category.

Most clothes and linens serve our daily needs. Few items of clothing or linens highlight a legacy story we hope to preserve. Even the dress I wore to Bethany's wedding is just a nice dress. The important memories of the wedding are captured in other items—photos, program, music CD.

Consequently the great majority of this stuff can be given or tossed. The more of those decisions made now, the more time loved ones will have to reflect on more important themes and stories. And, the more space you'll have for clothes you wear today. Plus, seriously, you deserve to have a new set of towels and sheets.

The Discovery Half-Day & Clothes and Linens

Few legacy stories live among our clothes and linens. Those that do can easily be set apart for quick discovery. The rest will likely be donated. Reducing nonessential volume today means less work for others down the road, and a cleaner closet for us today.

Most of us have unworn or wrong-sized clothes and extra linens that have accumulated over the years; double that for depression-era seniors. Estate sales often include piles of clothes and worn towels; and sheets in all sizes even though there was only one (single) bed. Did anyone else ever suggest Mom get new towels and crisp new matching sheets that fit her bed size and décor? We tried.

Over a lifetime, clothes and linens are easy to accumulate because:

- They are easy to store in out-of-site storage.
- Clothes and linens can be expensive to purchase.
- Needs vary by season or occasion.
- We can imagine some usefulness for this item or fabric – even if it's stained, worn out or the wrong size (does anyone else have a full wardrobe of paint clothes?)

For many of us letting go of seemingly useful items can feel like waste. Yet, loved ones who have to handle your clothes and linens as they grieve are likely to be hyper-stressed. From remembering Dad in that suit to smelling Mom's perfume on her scarf, clothing can pack a powerful emotional punch during cleanup. Less total stuff means they can actually sit with those emotions for a minute.

Definitely keep the items you love and use as well as those with special memories for you. Buy new stuff for today. But let the 20-year old clothes and unmatched sheets go.

How I Tackled Clothes and Linens

Match wardrobe and lifestyle

- Eliminate "when I lose 10 pounds" clothes and the spike heeled shoes your doctor won't let you wear.

- Donate professional clothes and shoes to charities that help people transition from poverty or tragedy into the workforce. On Mondays I smile thinking of a favorite suit making someone feel very good at her new job.

- Consign your clothes and shoes only if this process is fun for you. The dollars I made consigning a few fancy brand items did not match the time and effort I spent in the process. On the other hand, if you love the game, enjoy!

Match linens to beds

- How many beds do you have, in what size?

- The number of beds is also a hint as to how many overnight guests you regularly host. Reduce towel sets accordingly. Donate the rest to pet shelters.

Specialty or sentimental table clothes

- Set aside table linens that reflect a special holiday or theme, or hold sentimental value. Keep the ones you love and are likely to use or at least look at regularly. Donate the ones you didn't remember you had.

- Gift linens to family members if the linens:
  - Are in great shape
  - Are too special to you to donate just yet
  - Hold sentimental family meaning that can be shared in a note attached to the gift (e.g., "Your great-great grandmother designed and embroidered this table runner as a wedding gift to your great grandmother during the depression. The design signifies the strength of family.")

Treat yourself to something new!

True story: On her 100th birthday a great-aunt asked how long she might live. Why? Because if she was going to live at least another couple years she wanted to buy a new dress. Shortly before she passed away at 104 she said, "I'm so glad I bought that dress." Let the old stuff go. Then buy the dress.

The Payoff

- You'll like everything in the closet AND it fits.

- You'll re-experience the good feeling of a new set of sheets and matching, unraveled towels.

- You can imagine cute homeless puppies and kittens snuggling in your lovingly used donated towels and sheets.

- Clothes and linens rarely carry the cache that Grandma's cake plate might. Dealing with the stuff you aren't using truly means less stuff for your heirs to pack up and distribute.

Tips if You Get Stuck

- Donate unused, or gently used and unstained sheets and towels to a shelter for domestic abuse or trafficking victims, or a nonprofit that assists families who are establishing households after a disaster or homelessness. A clean set of sheets can provide a bit of comfort and care. Give the rest to a local veterinarian or animal shelter.

- Consider donating worn but unstained sheets to a daycare to cut up for paint shirts or costumes ☺

- Host a "Yours for the Taking" party. New (or near) retirees brings their contemporary, gently used (or never used) professional clothes for attendees to pick and choose from. In exchange, takers put an anonymous cash donation of their choice into a tin can marked for a preselected charity (e.g., Mr. Tony's second grade class, Evercare Senior Center). Online neighborhood communities such as NextDoor work great to promote this type of event.

- Remind yourself that eventually clothes and linens stored in the attic and basement are prime candidates for mold and mildew or worse, mousie condos. Letting go now means the item gets used by someone in need, and there is less icky cleanup waiting for you or your kids.

Do My Clothes and Linens Tell the Story I Want to Leave Behind? *Use this section to jot down items that highlight a legacy story or to note special items you intend to pass down. Are the items easy to find? Marked, organized? Note any special care required to preserve, showcase or pass down an item. Or use this space to doodle.*

Jewelry

The Stories Jewelry Leaves Behind

If you are a jeweler, professional or amateur, jewelry-making might be a story-rich theme. For the rest of us jewelry adds color and charm to other themes (hence the popularity of the "charm bracelet"). Perhaps you collected cufflinks; and their acquisition stories highlight a theme of travel. Maybe your multi-generation necklace collection speaks to a family theme. Or it's possible your exceedingly quirky-yet-high-end pieces point to a life theme about supporting emerging jewelry makers.

Whatever your jewelry tastes be, jewelry tends to fall in three broad buckets:

- Costume: your taste, no professional market value (rare vintage items aside)
- Gemstones: Typically insured on your homeowners policy (with appraisal)
- Memorabilia and Heirloom: Family-member jewelry

Jewelry may be tied to stories of family or relationships. Maybe you have an heirloom piece with documented monetary value or items that are the centerpiece for a legacy story (Great-Great Grandpa's ring from the old country). But most of our jewelry comes with mini stories. For example, "I got this bracelet on the train in 1965 on our way to visit my grandma." That's the whole story. Still, I'd like to distinguish certain "costume" items from items of no consequence.

Volume can be an added challenge. Because it takes up so little room, it is easy to over-accumulate jewelry. Plus jewelry is frequently passed down. But unless marked or somehow called out, cherished items disappear amidst the mundane.

Remember Grandma's costume jewelry box? Without a heads-up loved ones might not know there is something of interest or value until the whole lot has been tossed.

That brings us to value. Value is another wild card with jewelry. An item's value may be determined by purchase price or market value, by personal taste or current use, or by how the piece was acquired. My most cherished piece is a birthstone necklace from family. I also have a couple low-grade gemstone items I bought for myself that aren't "cherished" per se, but see regular wear. If I could only keep one I'd keep the necklace item because it holds the greater personal value.

The Discovery Half-Day & Jewelry

Several actions can minimize time spent digging through jewelry for cherished items:

- Clarify which items might have lasting value (personal or sentimental). Make it easy for loved ones to know where to look and you'll avoid losing "good" stuff among random costume jewelry.

- Group items together to minimize decisions. For example, put all costume jewelry in one location, one jewelry box, one drawer–with a sticky note saying "costume jewelry." Someone coming in will see this as one decision rather than 73 (or however many individual items you have).

- Collect formal or informal appraisals for items with monetary value. Keep the documents in a safety deposit box or fire box.

- Assign items that have monetary value or family significance in a will (or pre-gift).

How I Tackled Jewelry

I have costume jewelry, jewelry made (or gifted) by friends and family, special jewelry from my childhood, and a few items with, as the appraiser said, "sentimental value" passed down from relatives. I also have a couple items with a bit of monetary value. Currently I have everything I regularly wear in one location and items kept solely for sentimental reasons in another. Here was my process:

First, I gathered together cherished sentimental items that I never wear today. These items went in one zip lock bag with a small note describing each item's mini-story, typically a few words. One bag, one piece of paper.

Next, I gathered items together that I wear and included a brief note to distinguish sentimental items and those with potential market value from costume jewelry. One area, one piece of paper.

I collected informal appraisals for items I wanted to sell or donate (for a tax deduction). I put appraisal information in the fire safe until the item was sold or donated.

Finally, I looked through everything that remained and pulled out a few things I simply wanted to keep. A fun, local vintage store got first pick of everything else. Remaining items were donated to a teacher for craft projects.

The Payoff

- I can see what I have and I like, use and can find what I want!

- It was a blast donating a bunch of stuff to a local vintage store. As the owner and I looked through it some curious customers chimed in, and were elated when I said "would you like these?" The personal reward of that experience was far greater than the few dollars (and time and energy) I might have gotten at a garage sale or consignment shop.

- The kids got to weigh in on and request family jewelry (Grandpa's watch). Those decisions are done.

- Explanatory notes kept with my jewelry make it easy for anyone to quickly distinguish between items of monetary value and costume jewelry.

- Everything is in two easy-to-find locations; and there is relatively little.

- I can rest knowing the few items of value won't get accidentally tossed out.

Tips if You Get Stuck

- Donate costume jewelry to a vintage clothing store for displays.

- Consign pieces with a local clothing consignment shop that takes jewelry.

- Gift sentimental pieces now for birthdays or holidays.

- Donate to fundraisers for your favorite charity or GoFundMe campaign.

- Walk away. This is small stuff that takes up little room.

- Focus on the most valuable stuff. Briefly describe these items and save this note where it can be found (jewelry drawer, final will, safe deposit or fire box, even an e-file of important papers).

- Take pictures of cherished or valuable items then download the pics into a document; add brief descriptions including acquisition dates and any previous owners.

Does My Jewelry Tell the Story I Want to Leave Behind?
Use this section to jot down items that highlight a legacy story or to note special items you intend to pass down. Are the items easy to find? Marked, organized? Note any special care required to preserve, showcase or pass down an item. Or use this space to doodle.

ART

The Stories Art Leaves Behind

Similar to furniture, art provides a backdrop to our living space. Although each piece comes with its own mini story of how it came to us, much of the art we display (or store) simply adds beauty, joy and shape to our daily environment. On the other hand, if you are an art collector or an artist (or have a friend or family member who is), art may be its own theme or hold deeply meaningful legacy stories you'll want to preserve.

Often art speaks to personal taste and lifestyle while offering clues to ones themes and legacy stories. For example, all three of my professionally framed pieces are of young musicians. Other artwork connects to family, fun, or travel; each with potential legacy stories that connect to a theme. Take a moment to look around at your art. What themes or legacy stories are highlighted through your art?

Display the art that feeds your soul today.

The Discovery Half-Day & Art

You might have inherited an early sculpture by a recognized artist, yet your favorite piece may be a ceramic dog, or a drawing on the fridge from a special three-year old.

Separate items with meaning or that you simply like from those that, for whatever reason, still happen to live in your space. Next, take these two actions to simplify loved ones' decisions, reduce cleanup time, and maybe put a little cash in your pocket:

- Identify pieces of significant monetary value; I defined that as $500 or more (market and insured value). You might set a higher or lower baseline. Selling art takes work and time – and a willing buyer.

If you love the game go for it. But don't save lesser-priced art as monetary inheritance for loved ones. What you'll leave them is a job few will take up. Instead, focus on high-ticket items.

Get formal or informal appraisals and keep them together in a safety deposit box or fire box along with important original paperwork. Let loved ones know where this information is.

- Assign pieces of family significance or monetary value in your will or pre-gift them along with the item's history (where it originated, when it was acquired and/or passed down) and why it is being passed on to this individual.

How I Tackled Art

Most of my art is decorative. However, I do have a set of framed prints that carry sentimental value and speak to my music story. As a set, the prints have sufficient eBay value to warrant distinguishing them from random Pier One purchases, but not enough to pay for a formal appraisal.

So I did a Google search, printed off sample sale listings for each print and called it good. This information provides a ballpark market price and a couple art websites where these could be sold (or at least advertised). Even if my heirs choose to keep or donate these prints, this information may provide tax relief or help divide up items fairly.

Next, I updated my knick-knacks and wall art to reflect my current interests. I even bought a couple new items. This gave my place a fresh, new feel that even the preschool grandkids noticed.

Then I went through the remaining pieces and asked:
- Is this memorabilia? If so, do I *need* to save it for personal reasons or family politics?
- Is this an item I simply *want* to keep for now?

Every item that I neither needed nor wanted found its way to a new owner. I gave away stuff that had no particular meaning or value, offered items of sentimental value to the kids, and donated a few items with limited value to fundraisers (after giving the kids a chance to "bid").

The Payoff

- My home environment reflects who I am today.

- I learned what artwork (if any) the kids care about.

- My to-do list no longer includes "determine market value" for a heap of items, most of which were determined to hold only "sentimental value" which is fine. Now I know and can move on.

- Important documents and appraisals are done and in one location, saving loved ones the hours for research, calls and visits it took me to put all this together.

- Items of monetary value can be quickly sorted from everything else.

- Art pieces can confidently be donated or divided.

Tips if You Get Stuck

- Start small. Focus on a low-stress actions with a distinct beginning and end. Gathering market data online was that for me. I searched Google for specific artwork when I was already on the web.

- Stand at the entry to a room. Notice what you have. How does the space "feel"? Crowded? Fun? Calm? Where does your eye go? What do visitors notice? Does any of this no longer reflect who I am? Your answers to any of these questions can point to next steps.

- If you have works of minimum value that no one wants but you can't bring yourself to drop off at Goodwill, contact a small non-profit that might appreciate a donation of lovely art for their space. Any non-profit will do. One of my fun pieces is now in Mr. Tony's second grade classroom.

- Small museums that house pieces by an artist whose *original* work you own might be interested in a donation.

Does My Art Tell the Story I Want to Leave Behind? *Use this section to jot down items that highlight a legacy story or to note special items you intend to pass down. Are the items easy to find? Marked, organized? Note any special care required to preserve, showcase or pass down an item. Or use this space to doodle.*

SPECIAL COLLECTIONS

Heirlooms, Memorabilia and Collectibles

The Stories Special Collections Leave Behind

This section is longer than other categories because this stuff is harder to process than other categories. One reason is that special collections, especially stuff passed down, may relate to someone else's themes, someone else's story. You just happen to be holding onto it. And that takes time to process.

Stuff that doesn't reflect your themes or stories can easily distract from or confuse the stories that truly are your own. So, unless "duty" is a top five theme for you, separate the items that connect to your themes and stories and move the others along.

Conversations about special collections tends to center around heirlooms, memorabilia, and collectibles. I decided to group these together under the broad category of "Special Collections" because:

a) Each group may include items from multiple other categories (kitchen, art, and so forth).

b) Some items may fall under two or all three of these groups (e.g., Grandpa's extensive set of pristine 1960s rookie cards [collectible] he and Billy used to sort through together [memorabilia]).

c) Items tend to carry personal or monetary value, thus dispersal may be emotionally charged. No one cares who gets Mom's leftover paper plates. But who takes the sentimental cake plate, or the valuable model car collection, or love letters between grandparents during the war–that's another story.

The term "antique" is worth a quick mention.

I did not include antiques separately in this list because antiques appear in all three groups. Also the term antique is often used simply to describe something that is old.

Contrast that with the web definition of antique: *a **collectible** object such as a piece of furniture or work of art that **has a high value** because of its **considerable age***. Being old – of considerable age – is only one of the three (underlined) criteria that renders something an antique. And as we all know, just being old does not necessarily mean having monetary value.

My items were easily distinguished by common definitions (italics) to my stuff. Yours may require deeper distinctions.

***Heirlooms** – valuable objects that have belonged to one's family for several generations.*

- Items with potential monetary value or interest that once had a practical use (clay water jug circa 1900) or were a special gift (the rocker Great-Grandpa made Great-Grandma in the '30s), and were owned by someone important to my family who likely died before I was born.

- Cherished items from my upbringing, or from someone special to me from years back, that are no longer available (a 1953 ducky pull-toy that would fail multiple child safety hazards but the grandkids love).

Memorabilia – *objects kept or collected because of their historical interest [to me]; especially items associated with memorable people or events.*

- Items that spark a treasured memory and likely serve no other purpose.

- Items high on sentimental value with little or no market value (letters, cards, child drawings, certain gifts, special event programs and so forth).

Collectibles – *items that at one time were valued and sought by collectors and may or may not have much current monetary value.*

- Collectibles are distinct from hobby-like collections in how they are valued by the marketplace and more importantly, by the owner. Typically, collections are accumulated as a hobby for personal enjoyment (be it bottle caps or Beanie Babies), whereas collectibles are acquired as an investment.

The Discovery Half-Day & Special Collections

The thing about special collections is that they are, well, "special" to you but less so to the general public. A child's drawing, a photo mug, Grandma's beagle figurines, Grandpa's tools. Each special because it connects you to a person or event that is special to you. Taking time to highlight these items will help loved ones distinguish and save things hold special meaning.

For example, say you have a lantern carried by your great-grandfather from the old country (a final gift handcrafted by *his* father for the journey) and passed down, generation to generation as a symbol of light and hope. To you and family members long gone, that lantern is truly special. To the rest of us, not so much. To preserve its specialness for your family, you'll also need to preserve its history.

A term from our curator friends is useful here: provenance. Simply put, provenance is an object's history starting with the list of people who have owned the object over time. Without a clear understanding of where something came from and how it arrived in your attic, loved ones are likely to see unmarked items as one more thing to clear out. Few of us have the time or interest to decide item by item to separate items of value (to family or the market) from things that are mostly junk.

Consider integrating cherished, older items into holiday celebrations now. This is a particularly fun way to connect younger family members with important family stories and ethnic heritage.

If you have items with history that you hope future generations will embrace and preserve, list the owners as well as important dates and stories along its journey to today. Keep the list with the item. Better yet, record key information directly on the item using a soft pencil or Stabilo All pencil: "Great Grandma Ryan, Dublin circa 1895." That simple task could save loved ones hours of time and angst while preserving important items and family stories.

Special collections also carry emotional weight; if not they wouldn't be considered special. In particular, letting go of family memorabilia and heirlooms may come with feelings of grief and loss – yours and those felt on behalf of the ancestor who "would be heartbroken." When you provide a final goodbye to memorabilia and heirlooms on behalf of past generations, you minimize decisions for the next generation and get a gold star in the "took care our own stuff" category, because at this point, it is all your stuff.

To begin:

- Let go of anything that doesn't highlight one of YOUR themes or legacy stories or doesn't feed your life today.

- Identify and date heirlooms (garage sale stickers placed on the bottom work well for my stuff; check with a professional if you need archival quality solutions).

- Put like things together. Clearly mark boxes and include brief descriptions:
  o Memorabilia box with Grandma's ceramic cat set and Dad's baby shoes
  o Pre-1900 heirloom items from the Anderson side of the family
  o Complete collection of vintage dolls

That brings us to collectibles. Collectibles can present a particular challenge for the discovery half day. Those who've spent time, money and garnered enjoyment from building a collection of true collectibles often hope someone down the road will respect, care for and enjoy the collection as much as they did. Possibly. But probably not. If this is you and you have a recipient in mind, call him or her today and ask if he or she is truly interested in the collection. But first consider:

- Will the collection's size and storage requirements present a financial burden or space challenge for the recipient (and his or her immediate family?)

- Is it still of popular interest?

- Is it easy to dispense with or is there a cost involved?

- Is the collection really the "thing" you want for the loved one, or does it represent an experience you hope the collection will bring?

- Is there another way to celebrate the collection and its meaning with the potential recipient and then let it go–and perhaps use the money for something meaningful to you both? If, for example, you have a collection of old cars you might both show the cars at one final annual event, sell them, and use the proceeds to fly together to see the Indianapolis 500.

If you have collectibles you plan to keep forever:

- Collect what you love; love what you collect; when you're done let it go.

- Don't count on collectibles making money for you or your heirs.
  - o What's hot now might not be hot tomorrow

  - o Scarcity drives monetary value. Online marketplaces provide a global market where most collectibles are easily found.

  - o Avoid traps that make it hard to let go of collectibles, such as "I paid so much for this" or "I'm sure I can get X for this"

  - o Carefully consider costs to store and care for collectibles. Consider redistributing funds for a new hobby or other goals (e.g., college tuition, savings, trip to Bali).

How I Tackled Special Collections

Tackling special collections was fairly easy once I identified and separated memorabilia (most of my stuff) from heirlooms (a few items, most that already fell into other categories like jewelry and art) and collectibles (I currently had none).

I offered heirlooms to the kids. The remaining items are now marked and housed in their logical category (the cake plate is in the kitchen, the necklace is with the jewelry).

I emptied my memorabilia boxes and separated the items I want to keep. Then I took photos of everything else and downloaded the photos to a Word document which I emailed to the kids with brief descriptions and a timeline. Anything they didn't claim within the time frame was donated to a friend's fundraiser.

Finally I searched for information on certain items and collections to determine what, if anything, had monetary value–which in turn helped me decide next steps. This was a very time-consuming project but knowing what I actually had was worth it.

For the record, you know all that stuff others say and we tell ourselves has got to be worth something (meaning cash)? Most of it isn't. Plus the work to find a buyer (local or national), deliver it to the buyer, and the price we'll likely get gave me a whole new attitude toward a bunch of "good" stuff that I really didn't care much about. China and silverware come to mind.

The Payoff

- I gained closet space (and attic, basement, garage....)

- I found things I didn't know I had.

- Special items are clearly marked.

- Stories are highlighted using the best items.

- I realized that the connections I feel to these "cherished" items are *my* connections, my feelings. The kids nod politely when I talk about an item but they don't want to own it. Realizing this reduced the feeling that I needed to preserve this stuff for them. Preservation of stuff they don't care about is no longer my, albeit self-imposed, responsibility.

- Less time commitment, stress and decision-making for loved ones.

Tips if You Get Stuck

- Donate fun collectibles to a middle-schooler's garage sale. They will LOVE those Beanie Babies, have a ready market, and earn money for camp ☺

- Sell (or donate) items to an antique dealer.

- Look for similar items at a flea market to get a sense of true market value (and maybe connect with someone who might take some things off your hands).

- Use 12X12 plastic craft storage boxes to create memorabilia boxes for major legacy stories or for individual family members.

- Take a photo, download it to a Word document, write the story, and pass the item along.

- Walk away. These items carry tons of emotional weight. Do whatever it takes to bring your mind back to your space, your life. What do you want to do in your space, your life? Take those answers with you when you dig back in.

Do My Special Collections Tell the Story I Want to Leave Behind? *Use this section to jot down items that highlight a legacy story or to note special items you intend to pass down. Are the items easy to find? Marked, organized? Note any special care required to preserve, showcase or pass down an item. Or use this space to doodle.*

MONEY AND IMPORTANT DOCUMENTS
*And money-like stuff – insurance, bonds, bank accounts,
investments*

The Stories Money & Important Documents Leave Behind

Money was a common theme for past generations. Ancestors came to America to find wealth. Parents saved pennies and worked multiple jobs to make sure offspring got the education and experience needed to "get a good job" for "an easier life" which implied stable work with above average pay and regular raises. Inheritance was about how much money and big property was left behind.

Although baby boomers were raised to do the same, that wasn't the adult life most of us experienced. Jobs became obsolete, companies closed, divorce rates increased, the recession hit our savings, college costs soared. For most of us money will not be among the top five themes we leave behind.

However, this category goes far beyond basic acquisition of funds. As such, there are ample opportunities to demonstrate themes such as care, love or order by taking steps to pull this stuff together–possibly something we've been meaning to do for ourselves for a long time.

Money, important documents, and money-like stuff includes all the practical, crucial items (and funds) loved ones may need to find (burial plot deed) or access (bank accounts) immediately following our demise. While these are rarely thought of as "things" one might leave behind, thoughtfully putting money and important documents in order now (a) puts you at ease knowing things are set up the way you want them, and (b) will avoid added stress at the height of a loved one's grief.

Money, important documents and money-like stuff fall under one category because they are **time sensitive**. Social security card, tax documents, bills, mortgage papers, life insurance, financial accounts, and other documents will need to be found and filed—some immediately.

Insurance must be claimed and cancelled. Accounts may even be frozen, making it a challenge to pay funeral expenses or final bills unless you've planned ahead. Plus, once a public death certificate is filed identity thieves and other unscrupulous opportunists look for ways to wreak havoc on someone's life savings.

And, the more time loved ones must spend here, the harder it will be to face your living space.

The Discovery Half-Day and Money & Important Documents

This was a particularly stressful experience when my dad died. He honestly believed he had things in order. He did not. A big challenge was his lifelong unwillingness to share information about money, insurance, and the like with anyone. Not even his attorney or best friend had any clues. As a result, many significant decisions (and personal financial commitments) were made without a clear understanding of their resources. This pattern continued for months causing relentless personal stress; stress that didn't have to be. Please don't do this to your loved ones.

Applying the discovery half-day concept to money or money-like stuff is about kindness, transparency, and simplification.

And whether it is money (e.g., cash, personal bank accounts) or money-like stuff (401ks, pensions, investments, life insurance, anything else with a beneficiary designation, real-estate or other property) loved ones will devote whatever time it takes to collect these funds because in this case time IS money. Don't make loved ones look for stuff. Do the hard work to identify *what you have and where it is* so loved ones don't have to.

For example, many of us have held multiple jobs, each with its own version of a 401k or savings plan. Companies merge, fund names change, small accounts are forgotten. Some of those companies may not even exist anymore. Loved ones won't know where to start and might miss out on hidden funds. Documenting information about current accounts will save them countless hours of searching and worry.

Then let loved ones know **now** what exists, where it is, how to access it, who has access, and any procedures required to access it. This can all be done without revealing personal details (such as in the will) that you'd like to save for after you're gone. Reducing the time needed to identify and collect funds significantly decreases stress and worry.

I can summarize this in three words:

1. Organize
2. Document
3. Share

How I Tackled Money & Important Documents

Unlike photos or jewelry, my money and documents had no legacy stories. However, and this is important, *organizing them and making funds easy for loved ones to access did*. The last thing I wanted to leave behind was the expensive and incredibly stressful hunting expedition for essential documents and funds I experienced when my dad died. I decided my legacy story around money and important documents would be how simple I made this task and how quickly loved ones could access funds.

Here are the steps I took to organize, document and share information about money, important documents and money-like stuff. Most steps I could take myself. Some involved a professional. Each step increased my confidence that my funds and important documents are in good order for loved ones. And, I marked several big tasks off my to-do list!

1. *Organize*

- Consider merging similar accounts.

- Have a well-marked filing system for quick retrieval.

- Keep a current list of passwords and let loved ones know where it is.

- Keep originals in a safe deposit box or other single, secure location.

- Share the location of these documents with your loved ones.

- Include insurance, bonds, bank accounts, investments, trust accounts, and the like. Add contact information for applicable agents or representatives.

- Update account beneficiaries, POD (payable-on-death), TOD (transfer on death) and other designations.

- Gather documents or critical information loved ones might not be aware of that might be needed to collect benefits, confirm citizenship or apply for certain scholarships. Examples include military records, birth certificates, heritage or immigration records, baptismal records–any official record that is used to collect benefits, confirm citizenship, or apply for certain scholarships.

2. *Document*

- Create a list of assets and important information (insurance policies, account numbers, contacts; loan information), where accounts are, types of account, the beneficiaries and current values. Update annually.

- Create a Will
    - Have one; the clearer the better.

    - Your executor or personal representative will be in charge of settling your estate on your behalf. Let your loved ones know who this is and make sure the individual is willing, capable, and up to the task (will they do it, can they do it, should they do it).

    - Work with an attorney to set up stuff for easy transfer (payable on death accounts, updated beneficiaries on assets, etc.)

    - Have conversations NOW about specifics to reduce questions and decisions, and to resolve issues or re-evaluate decisions.

- Complete a living will/health care surrogate form and a financial power of attorney.
  - o Clear, complete documentation may facilitate financial transactions and streamline health care, minimizing emotional decisions that your loved ones may face.

- Pre-arrangements for funeral.
  - o Include cemetery plot deeds and other obscure documents a grieving loved one might prefer not to hunt for in the days after you pass.

3. *Share*

- Share the list with your heirs, or tell them who has the list. This information is especially important for those who may be asked to deal with your body and/or make decisions about a funeral. Heirs with a roadmap avoid wasting precious time hunting down important assets that may be needed for funeral expenses. Keep extra copies in a safe deposit or fire box.

The Payoff

- There is an awareness of total assets.

- You're able to confidently and thoughtfully make decisions about current expenses and gifts.

- It is easy to track and manage your total assets.

- Loved ones will feel secure that there are no lost, forgotten or hidden funds.

- There should be a relatively quick turnaround of life insurance proceeds.

- Loved ones will have quick access to funds for immediate funeral expenses.

- You'll reduce the chance your funds could be tapped by thieves targeting the recently deceased.

Tips if You Get Stuck

- Honestly I don't have an alternative approach for money, documents and money-like stuff. I suppose it could all be given away and you could move into your grandson's basement, but that's less "alternative" and more "what were you thinking." Just pull things together the best you can and let loved ones know where money, documents and money-like stuff are. Period.

- Take it slow. Group like things together. For example, it took me almost a year to merge my two bank accounts into one institution. It wasn't complicated; I just needed time to decide which institution best served my needs.

- Confirm account balances online. For me that meant setting up online accounts, which in itself was progress. Make a list of the websites, your account numbers and passwords (updated as necessary). Keep in a secure location that loved ones can access (or keep a paper copy in a fire safe for which they have the key).

Do Money & Important Documents Tell the Story I Want to Leave Behind? *Use this section to jot down items that highlight a legacy story or to note special items you intend to pass down. Are the items easy to find? Marked, organized? Note any special care required to preserve, showcase or pass down an item. Or use this space to doodle.*

RESIDENTIAL AND NON-RESIDENTIAL PROPERTY

The Stories Residential & Non-Residential Property Leave Behind

As with money, important documents, and money-like stuff, residential and non-residential property can be a time-consuming, stressful task. However, items in this category are a bit less time sensitive. Time may still be of the essence for personal or monetary reasons. Again, time and stress spent on this stuff means less time discovering and reflecting on the positive legacy stories you hope they'll see.

Residential and non-residential property speak to themes such as adventure, travel, wanderlust, home, family, and so forth. Included is anything that involved a legal contract to buy, requires a title to sell, or requires a license to operate.

Examples include:

- House, condo, townhome
- Motorhome
- Cars & trucks
- Motorcycles
- Boats
- Snowmobiles
- Farm equipment
- Cabin
- Time-share
- Grandma's farm that you inherited and own jointly with siblings

The Discovery Half-Day and Residential & Non-Residential Property

Transferring, dividing or selling residential and non-residential property is outside the Discovery Half-Day for sure. However, there are ample opportunities to simplify loved ones' decisions and the disposition of these items.

- Gather and keep important documents together (purchase information, deed, titles, insurance and so forth). Confirm your documents are current and nothing is missing.

- Be honest with yourself. You acquired that road racer for a reason and it served you well. *But does it still?* Does your current use warrant keeping it? If not, let it go now. Would you rather keep the farm even though you are rarely there? Or would you prefer to be remembered as the grandparent who dealt with the farm before he, well, "bought the farm"?

- Ask if an heir would like to buy the item or receive it as a gift (to be added to the "what Billy already got" list). Otherwise, sell it and add the funds to savings, a child's inheritance, grandchild's college fund, or sail around the world. It is your money. Use it for something that reflects your interests and long term values. If that means keep it, then keep it.

How I Tackled Residential & Non-Residential Property

- Personally I own one car and one small condo, period. I need them both. I took two actions to simplify transfer or sale.

    o I made sure the condo deed and car title were together in a safe location that is known and accessible for my kids.

    o When I updated my will I had the attorney add language and legal documents that will automatically transfer the condo to my heirs to facilitate a quick sale.

The Payoff

- You'll save money otherwise used for maintenance, storage, annual license and tabs, property taxes, fees, and squirrels (for some reason there are always squirrels).

- You can do some really rewarding legacy-type things with that money; or enjoy a little more financial security; or have a fabulous vacation.

- Important documents are in order, saving countless hours (and fees) tracking these down.

- Your heirs will avoid a stressful waiting time before they can implement their decision about the property.

Tips if You Get Stuck

- Depending on the shape it's in, consider donating vehicles that need repair to a trade school or work program. A friend donated his well-used houseboat to a local Boy Scout troop for a boat rebuilding project, and got quite the tax deduction.

- Decide to give yourself six months for personal observation. Keep track of how often you visit property or use the item FOR FUN versus for maintenance. Keep track of any related expenses including transportation back and forth.

  At the end of your data collection period add up all those hours and the money you spent. Ask yourself, if someone handed me this amount of cash and time and I could do anything with it, what would I do? Maybe do that.

Does My Residential & Non-Residential Property Tell the Story I Want to Leave Behind? *Use this section to jot down items that highlight a legacy story or to note special items you intend to pass down. Are the items easy to find? Marked, organized? Note any special care required to preserve, showcase or pass down an item. Or use this space to doodle.*

YOUR CHOICE CATEGORY

Everyone has stuff that demands its own category. This section is for yours. I've included a few starter questions.

What Story do I Want to Tell with _____?
What themes appear in stuff from this category?

The Discovery Half-Day & _____ *Actions I can take to minimize decisions loved ones will need to make after I'm gone.*

How I Can Tackle_____?

Who might want this?

How much work would it be to find out?(e.g., call Billy, conduct a global search of antique dealers)

How easy or hard it would be to deliver the item?

First steps:

- *Email loved ones a list of items that are on the chopping block. Include a deadline for a decision and a requested retrieve-by date.*
- *Post pictures on Facebook of items you "hate to just give away" but would donate to a "good home". Include pick-up or delivery parameters.*
- *Likewise with special items for out-of-towners I've sent photos with parameters for decision and pickup.*
- *Family garage sales are also effective. Everything remaining by close of business is donated elsewhere.*

The Payoff

- *How would addressing this stuff make life better today? "I can stop thinking about it" is an answer.*

- *How would life be better down the road? A simple "one less thing to make decisions about, argue over, think about" is a fine answer.*

Tips if You Get Stuck

- *Go wild. Start with the craziest idea that pops in your head for dealing with this category of stuff. Work backwards from there.*

- *Give yourself a break. Tackle something clear and easy — like assembling boxes, or laundry, or taking out the garbage. Go to a movie. Walk with a friend. Ride your motorcycle in the wind. Visit a new coffee shop or restaurant.*

- *Mention the item/category to a co-worker in conversation. You never know who might have a great idea.*

Does _____ Tell the Story I Want to Leave Behind? *Use this section to jot down items that highlight a legacy story or to note special items you intend to pass down. Are the items easy to find? Marked, organized? Note any special care required to preserve, showcase or pass down an item. Or use this space to doodle.*

Chapter Five

LIVING AMONG YOUR BEST STORIES

*"I've learned that people will forget what you said, people
will forget what you did, but people will never forget how
you made them feel."*
Maya Angelou

MY LIFE TODAY

Much has changed since I began this journey. My home reflects *my* themes and favorite stories, my current lifestyle, and my interests. I like the way it feels when I walk in the door; and I feel good about how others respond to my space.

I've identified the stories, themes and messages I hope to pass on and taken steps to preserve them. I have peace of mind knowing that, even if today is my last day, things are in good order for my loved ones.

But the biggest surprise is the freedom and flexibility I feel each day. Every time I prioritized a legacy story, chose a single item from a collection, or gathered crucial documents in a single location, space opened up; physical space and psychological space.

I can't explain it. But I feel it–in an unexpected deep breath, a gentle quieting of the mind. Like a storm is starting to subside.

It feels like starting out again but with life's best lessons and my best stuff in plain view; reminders I've done all right in spite of the hard times–and a sense that whatever lies ahead will be all right too. And it feels great.

In short:

- I have time, space and energy for new interests and the people I love.

- I share the stories that have the most meaning to me.

- I can make changes quickly to match current interests and needs.

- I spend retirement being retired, however I define that today.

- I keep only the stuff that preserves important stories or feeds current lifestyle and interests.

AM I DONE?

Being done with our stories and cleanup is like being done with laundry. As long as we are engaged in life, there will be more to do. Probably not new themes, but new stories and stuff within those themes.

Putting things in order right now and taking steps to preserve the stories you want to pass along will get you 90% there. And, you'll free up energy, time and money to recognize and embrace new, enriching opportunities when they arise.

Instead of striving toward "done" I work to maintain the progress I've achieved and keep on track as things change. For starters:

- I strive to maintain an environment that reflects my style and current interests.

- I keep important documents up to date (easy now that like things are actually together).

- I update the individualized photo albums every few months.

- And I keep an eye out for stuff that no longer needs to live in my space. Each action taken in this regard is considered a win.

And I look for moments that suggest I'm on the right track. Here are some favorites:

- I walk in the front door, smile and breathe (versus think "what task must I do next").

- The grandkids are drawn to their photo albums (""Mom!", "Me!")

- I can answer with confidence when asked "Do you have…" (and can find it right away).

- My adult children mention me to friends whose parents are struggling with stuff.

- I no longer have to choose between walking with a friend and sorting through stuff.

RESOURCES THAT INSPIRED

Three recent books provided inspiration. Two advocate for simplicity not as a "should do" but as a means to embrace the best of our lives and shape the stories we leave for loved ones. The third is a great example of capturing a legacy story. I've also included two organizations worth noting that help individuals preserve their stories.

> ➤ *The Gentle Art of Swedish Death Cleaning – How to free yourself and your family from a lifetime of clutter* by Margareta Magnusson (Simon and Schuster, 2018). This charming little book offers a distinct take on how and why to put one's home in order while we can.

> ➤ *Soulful Simplicity – How living with less can lead to so much more* by Courtney Carver (Tarcher Perigree, 2017). Carver, a well-known blogger on minimalism, describes the events and path that led her and her family to a simpler and happier life. Using a calm, clear voice Carver offers practical, personal suggestions to embrace what matters most.

> ➤ *Gumma's Family Recipes* by Kara Hefner (CreateSpace, 2018). This lovely book began as a way to record the legacy (and recipes) of a Grandma who loved to cook for family. It is a great example of capturing a legacy story for generations to come.

> ➤ *StoryCorps* seeks to increase compassion and understanding across generations and cultures through sharing of personal stories. Participants invite a loved one to a mobile StoryCorps recording site to share a 40-minute meaningful conversation, later archived with the Library of Congress. Edited versions are available on their website https://storycorps.org/

- ➢ *MemoryWell* uses professional journalists to hand-craft individual life stories using photos, video, and a brief phone interview. The result is a hand-crafted story of 400-800 words. https://www.memory-well.com/

- ➢ *The Art of Storytelling/Pixar in a Box* In this entertaining behind-the-scenes (free) video course, Pixar artists share insights about how to tell a story and make characters come to life. So. Much. Fun. https://www.khanacademy.org/partner-content/pixar/storytelling

FINAL WORDS

As baby boomers we think long and hard about our legacy. We hope to leave the world a better place for future generations; to be remembered as someone who embraced life and did right by others–especially those we held most dear. When all is said and done, how do we want loved ones to feel? What stories do we hope they tell?

As life changes so will our stories and our stuff. Keeping a relatively short attention window in mind can help prioritize what to highlight, keep for current use (or just because), or move along.

By acting today to highlight cherished stories and minimize cleanup decisions you'll create a legacy loved ones will cherish–and a life that is yours to live today.

Remember:

What you do matters. You matter. Your stories matter.

Let them shine.

EPILOGUE: A STORY OF STUFF

This is the story of baby boomers Kathy and Mike and all their stuff. As with many stuff-laden baby boomers, the story actually began a long time ago in a land far, far away with a little girl named Esther...

Once upon a time there lived a little girl named Esther. Faced with war, famine and a growing sense of despair Esther and her parents left their homeland to come to America. They brought the clothes on their backs and a few prized possessions packed in a large wooden chest hand-carved by Esther's grandfather to whom they had bid a sad (and final) farewell. Each item held stories of home.

As the family settled in to American life they gathered and made essential, useful things; clothes, tools, a bed, a table and so forth. Each new item served as a symbol of hard work and success. Each item was designed to last a lifetime or longer.

Esther grew up and married a young soldier named Edgar. Esther brought her "hope chest"–a heavy wooden chest full of dowry items such as a handmade quilt, table linens, towels, dishware, and family baby clothes; the basics for a proper home. These items were not "starter" items in today's terms. These were intended to last forever because that's how it was back then.

Soon Esther and Edgar had children including a daughter they named Dorothy. Esther and Edgar gathered more things. Suddenly the depression hit followed by a second world war. Times were tough. Everything was in short supply. Esther and Edgar taught their children to make do with very little and to appreciate what they had. By the time life turned around Dorothy and her siblings were young adults, eager to never go without again and fearful of letting go of anything–just in case.

It was now the 1950's. Dorothy met and married Stan, a young man eager to make his (and his parents') dreams come true. Post-war times were good. Stuff was plentiful and a mark of success. New-fangled stuff like TVs, swanky furniture, appliances, and cool cars were all the rage. Dorothy and Stan worked hard to build a lovely home with room for lots of stuff for their four "Baby Boom" kids: Kathy, Susie, Mary and Stan Jr. The kids had toys, clothes, transistor radios and board games; and were expected to take good care of everything so the stuff could last "forever".

Time moved on. Stan Jr. went off to Vietnam, Susie went to nursing school, Mary ran off to California, and Kathy–the eldest–met a nice guy named Mike and got married. And stuff was gathered and saved. And everyone needed more storage space.

More time passed. It was now the 1980's. Kathy and Mike had kids and their kids had stuff. Lots of stuff. New stuff. Essential stuff. Extra stuff. Cool stuff. "He who dies with the most toys wins" was the motto of the times.

Sad, but true, eventually Esther and Edgar died along with other relatives. With the passing of each relative Dorothy and Stan inherited stuff; big stuff, little stuff, useful stuff, immovable stuff, antique stuff, curious stuff, broken stuff, stuff passed down from relatives they'd never met. If it had ever been owned by a family member it stayed in the family. Dorothy and Stan added on to their house.

Time passed. Everyone collected more things. There were birthdays, holidays, sales too good to pass up, stuff acquired for today and stuff to serve an imagined need "someday".

And then the story shifted.

Kathy and Mike's kids grew up and went off to college.

The kids did **not** take their stuff to college because they bought new stuff, different stuff. Even after they graduated and (eventually) moved out on their own, their stuff from childhood and college remained with Kathy and Mike in case they might need it/want it someday.

It wasn't long before Kathy and Mike became grandparents–which meant more stuff. Dorothy and Stan grew old and frail. As the eldest, Kathy became the first stop for Dorothy and Stan's stuff (and everything they'd inherited) as did husband Mike for his parents' stuff.

Kathy tried to help them downsize but as we already know, Dorothy and Stan were raised during the depression by immigrant parents, which means every single item is deemed worthy of a new, loving home; preferably within the family or to a known recipient. Conversations frequently began with:

"That belonged to your great aunt…"

"It has a few dings but somebody can surely fix this right up good as new!"

"I paid so much for this!"

"Someone must be able to use this!"

"You never know when you might need one of these!"

"Wouldn't Shane like to have this?"

Last summer Dorothy died, leaving Kathy to sort through everything with her elderly father.

Kathy and Mike shift time between work, care of aging parents (hers and his), care of grandchildren, and dealing with the piles of stuff in their house. They want to be loving and kind "good kids" to their aging parents but they never signed up to become the reluctant keepers of several generations' worth of stuff.

Kathy and Mike are overwhelmed. And tired. They have a nagging sense that all this stuff is getting in the way of the life they hoped to lead by now. And their stories are getting lost in the shuffle.

They've had enough.

Kathy and Mike see two options:

a) Leave the ever-increasing stuff bomb for their offspring to face upon Kathy and Mike's demise which means living with it in the meantime–which makes it *their* story (two thumbs down), or

b) Refocus on their own lives and legacy stories; and be the line in the sand–the buck where things stop–the end of the road for the stuff no one in their family actually wants.

They chose "b" and booked a vacation for just the two of them–with no cell phones. It was a good start. It is their turn.

.

ACTIVITIES

This section includes short-answer activities, book club questions, and a notes page for whatever you want. Each activity is independent from the others. Some are simply different approaches to the same end–helping you uncover your legacy themes and stories.

Use the activities that speak to you. The first two are especially enjoyable to do with a friend.

Have fun!

HOLLYWOOD CALLS!

1. Use pencil. Things change.
2. Answer quickly. Don't get stuck in your head.
3. Come back later and reflect. What fits? Has changed?
4. Have fun. There is no judgment, no right/wrong. Play!

The Academy Award Goes To...

Imagine Hollywood is making a movie about your life. The director, writer and set designer are on their way to your home.

1. Stand at the entrance to your home. What do you hope they notice? A thing (chair), a favorite area (custom kitchen), a feeling (warmth), a smell (fresh apple pie), or something else?

2. Walk around your home. Name three storylines you hope they highlight in the film and three items they should use in the set:

   **Storylines**   _**Items for the Set**_

3. Is an important theme, storyline or item not visible?

4. Name three characteristics that describe how you hope to be portrayed.

5. Choose the actor who will portray you in the film:

   Actor: Why:

What stands out about your answers? Any surprises? Say more about the actor you chose. Do you relate to a specific character or to the actor him or herself?

What's the title of your movie?

LEGACY STORIES – THEN & NOW

Here's a quick exercise to help you uncover legacy stories.

1. Imagine you are flying to attend your a high school reunion, the first you've attended since you graduated in, well, the age of Aquarius (give or take). You've had no contact with classmates since graduation. What stories and characteristics shape their memory of you? List these under THEN. What stories since then shape who you are today (stories that you'd like your classmates to know)? List these under NOW.

THEN   NOW

2. Look at your lists.

- Are the themes consistent or different?

- Did you recall stories you'd like to resurrect and share with loved ones?

- Are there stories in between then and now that tell of an important personal journey in your life? Maybe you overcame horrible shyness or conquered a learning disability. Maybe you are simply a stronger, better you. (For inspiration re-watch *Romy and Michele's High School Reunion*).

3. In the space below, copy your "NOW" list from above. Next, under "LOVED ONES" name three stories or characteristics that summarize how you are thought of *by loved ones* today (or would like to be remembered). Are the lists the same or different?

   If the lists are different, the NOW column may reflect how you wish to be known professionally or publically. In contrast, the LOVED ONES column may reflect how you wish to be remembered by those who know you best, have walked with you along your path, and are most important in your life.

   Preserve those stories first.

   <u>NOW</u>   <u>LOVED ONES</u>

COMPLETE THIS STATEMENT

Thinking about a theme or legacy story you'd like loved ones to remember, complete the following statements:

1. I hope my friends and family will remember me as:

    Or, I hope I've made a difference for:

2. I believe they will remember because...(describe how your life reflects this value, characteristic or accomplishment; name related experiences you and a loved one shared):

3. The tangible stuff that tells this story includes:

4. Is this story obvious in my space? Does the current setup tell a clear and compelling story?

STAND AND CONSIDER

Stand back and survey your stuff. Look at one room (kitchen), one set of stuff (books), one item (heirloom vase), or do a mental scan of everything.

1. What themes, personal values or characteristics are reflected in your stuff? (e.g., family, adventure, art, entertaining)

2. Which themes, personal values or characteristics do you consider important to pass on; to be part of your legacy?

3. Which items tell those stories efficiently and meaningfully?

PRESERVING YOUR THEMES AND STORIES

Use these questions to assess how discoverable your themes and stories are today. Track ideas and progress. Use pencil!

1. Items that highlight this theme.
    Ex. (family theme) photos, play area, memorabilia

2. Are key stories easily discovered?

3. Are stories inviting?

4. Are stories brief?

5. Actions to preserve this theme.

COFFEE CHAT
A conversation guide

Use this activity to facilitate an initial conversation about life, legacy and stuff between you and the person(s) likely to inherit your stuff. This might be an adult child, niece or nephew, friend, neighbor, or even a charity.

Meet at a coffee shop; or anywhere besides home. Otherwise it is too easy to start sorting before reaching a good understanding of each person's goals and interests.

- What are each person's hopes for this conversation?
  - Share time and a good cup of coffee
  - Start a conversation about life, legacy and/or stuff
  - Make a concrete action plan
  - Just chat

- Do you have an immediate or near-term goal?
  - Move to a smaller place
  - Declutter, simplify current environment
  - Gift special items (e.g, heirlooms or items listed in a will)
  - Preserve legacy stories
  - Share information about (or access to) important documents or accounts

- What type of help do you want?
  - Help making yes/no decisions
  - Help sorting, packing, delivering items
  - Just listening

- What is your timeline?

- What can the other person comfortably offer given his or her own stage in life including:
    o Work and family responsibilities
    o Health
    o Personal long-term plans (e.g., travel, simplify, move to another state)

- Which of your needs match with what the other person can offer?

- What needs must be met by someone else?

- What are 1-2 initial tasks each of you can do this month that support your goal?

- Plan next steps (including dates) such as:
    o A follow-up conversation
    o Others to contact
    o Decisions to be made
    o A timeline for completing initial tasks

- Express appreciation both ways

BOOK CLUB QUESTIONS

Use these questions to start a group discussion.

1. Does this book speak to a challenge you face (or expect to face in the coming years)?

2. If so, have you experienced any roadblocks to action? What has helped you move forward?

3. What did you find most helpful about this book?

4. What feelings did this book evoke for you?

5. Share a favorite quote or idea from the book. Why did this quote stand out?

6. How do you want to be remembered? Share one story you hope to preserve. This can be about a hobby, vocation, a personal characteristic or value or belief system. The floor is yours.

7. Describe 2-3 items that tell that story.

8. If you got the chance to ask the author one question, what would it be?

9. How might you apply something from this book to preserve your stories?

10. What else have you read on this topic, and would you recommend these books to others?

NOTES PAGE

Use this page to track actions taken, ideas for gifting, sketch plans for a getaway.
This is your space.

ABOUT THE AUTHOR

Laura H. Gilbert holds a Ph.D. in Educational Psychology and is a licensed attorney in Minnesota. Laura currently divides her time between long-distance caregiving, volunteering, biking, and creating memories with grandchildren. Laura is also a lifelong advocate for higher education. Her earlier works include *Our Plan: A Family-Centered Approach to Paying for College, How to Save $50,000 on College, Graduate School on a Budget,* and *Back to School for Grownups.*

Made in the USA
Lexington, KY
09 February 2019